They Called Me Retard
What is your foundation?

GORDON WALSH
with Ken Walker

They Called Me Retard
Copyright © 2023 by Gordon Walsh

All rights reserved. No part of this publication may be reproduced, distributed, or transmitted in any form or by any means, including photocopying, recording, or other electronic or mechanical methods, without the prior written permission of the publisher or author, except in the case of brief quotations embodied in critical reviews and certain other noncommercial uses permitted by copyright law.

Although every precaution has been taken to verify the accuracy of the information contained herein, the author and publisher assume no responsibility for any errors or omissions. No liability is assumed for damages that may result from the use of information contained within.

Library of Congress Control Number:		2021919620
ISBN-13:	Paperback:	978-1-64749-627-2
	ePub:	978-1-64749-628-9

Printed in the United States of America

GoTo Publish

GoToPublish LLC
1-888-337-1724
www.gotopublish.com
info@gotopublish.com

Introduction

One of the unique things I have discovered in my time as a pastor and leader in the military is, people do not let go of their past. Unfortunately, this past becomes part of our foundation. There have been many times that I have talked to someone about an issue they are going through at the present time, and by the end of our discussion, they are revealing something that happened to them as a child. They are holding on to this one or more offenses for a lifetime. One good example is when I was talking to two elderly people, one was in their eighties and the other in their seventies, and at the end of our session, they are talking about their childhood and the trauma they experienced.

I, too, had childhood trauma and despicable things happen to me. Consequently, I carried these traumas into my adult life, and it became part of my foundation. My story is interwoven throughout this book, but each chapter is about foundations. As a child, I was molested (foundation of intimacy). I was unable to read well, second-grade level in the eighth grade, and still struggle with spelling (foundation of learning), and many more things happened to me. All this story is woven throughout this book. All the things that happened to me became part of my foundation.

This traumatic experience I went through became part of my foundation. This is where the foundation of the apple tree comes in; it explains what happens to people as they experience trauma in their life. One thing you should remember is that not every one's response to trauma or a traumatic experience the same way; we are all different and our response to a situation is also different. I experienced this in the Army and helping soldiers through some traumatic events. Four soldiers could go through the same thing in battle, and all four will handle their situation and their experience differently; some will have difficulty with it and need help, some are just fine (yes, some will bottle it up and years later have issues). What I am saying is this traumatic event will affect everyone differently, and we should not minimize the event. I know for myself I did not talk about being molested to anyone until I was in my forties, and even then, it was with my wife. I remember the second time I publicly shared my trauma, being molested, was when I was going through my residency for my master's degree with Northwest

University. We all were in a room together introducing ourselves. The professor told us to introduce ourselves and tell a little bit about our past. I was about the eighth or ninth person to share my story, and I remember before it was my turn; everyone was telling their life story, from childhood to present time. I was getting so nervous, my heart was pounding out my chest. I was sweating and thinking to myself, I don't want to tell my life story, not here, not today. I was running my life story through my head over and over again. When it was my turn, I was crying profusely, I could not stop. I told my life story and was so scared (big bad Green Beret, crying like a baby and scared, not really who I was) I could not even talk. I don't think anyone understood a word I said, but they just looked at me and afterward, people gave me comfort.

Most everyone has gone through some type of trauma in their life, and this book is about helping others or helping someone who can help someone. I have had a lot of traumatic experiences in my life as a young child, and I did not let that define me. I cannot change my past; however, I do have control over my future and the choices I make. This book is a Christian book, and I am a pastor, but I did not want only Christians to read this book. If you do not believe in Jesus Christ, then do not read the Christian passages or just read them as good advice. You latterly could read chapter 1, 2 (chapter 2 so you can understand trauma and how it affects our lives), 6, 10, and the one chapter you relate to. Yes, I believe all the book is good reading and encouraging; however, you do not have to read chapter 1, 2, 3, 4, etc. in order; you can read chapter 1, 2, 8, and 10 first, for example.

I pray this book finds you well and you are helped and encouraged. The reason I called the book *They Called Me Retard* is because kids did call me that and my inability to read still is part of my foundation. I always struggled in school and never thought of myself as intelligent, despite having a two master degrees, one in ministry and the other in leadership. I still have to pinch myself thinking, *Do I really deserve this, and am I qualified to be at this level of education?* The one trait I do have is determination and being goal-oriented (chapter 9). I have always set goals and have accomplished most all of them. It may take me more time, but I will complete it. The real issue is how we learn. Albert Einstein said, "Everyone is a genius. But if you judge a fish by its ability to climb a tree, it will live its whole life believing that it is stupid." Everyone has the ability to learn, but we do not learn the same way and have the same talents. When I was a child, the educators said I had a learning disability. I was the fish trying to climb a tree, and because of that, I did not find myself worthy; I thought I was stupid.

I hope this book helps you or someone you know could use help. Remember, we may be shaped by our past, but we are not defined by our past. Go and be life as you want your life to be, stop doing life, but be life.

CHAPTER 1
The Foundation of Family

Although the attack occurred in my childhood, the taunt carried a sting that lasts to this day. The words carried more of an impact than the bullets that used to whiz by my head during my days as a Green Beret with the United States Army Special Forces unit at Fort Lewis (currently Joint Base Lewis-McChord). Getting quickly categorized, stereotyped, and ridiculed as a child inflicts more damage than many people are aware of or even willing to acknowledge. Millions carry around childhood baggage for years—some all the way to their grave. Even in my late forties, I still deal with personal issues. Not only because of the labels others put on me, but the chaos that ruled my life until I reached the age of fifteen and refused yet another move to another dead-end small town.

"Hey, retard!" yelled my detractor.
I winced, then I felt a storm gathering inside.

Now, it wasn't like I hadn't heard this crude nickname before. Just try struggling to read beyond the first grade and see how quickly some harsh slang rolls off another unfeeling person's lips. None of my elementary school teachers seemed capable of picking up on my learning style. By the time I entered the third grade, my inability to read sent me to a parochial school for mentally and physically challenged children with special needs (handicapped in my day). Although I returned to a traditional elementary setting the next year, they put me in a special needs class designed for children with physical or mental disabilities. Since I was unable to read, they classified me as *mentally challenged*.

While more than one student had aimed thrown the "retard" label in my direction, this particular day of fourth grade, it struck a nerve. I wasn't very big, but I was fast (later, when I enrolled in karate class, my feet and hands made me an expert student!). Today marked the first demonstration of my hand speed. Tearing off in his direction, I popped him with a roundhouse right, and standing over him as I took satisfaction in settling more than one score, I spat, "I have a name." I whipped him so hard, it changed his vocabulary (or least his vocabulary toward me); he never called me retard again.

Although that is all I said out loud, inside the fury roared. Every time kids called me a name or teachers labeled me hopeless, it felt like a knife tearing into my heart. I wanted to stand and shout, "I am *not* mentally challenged. I am *not* a *retard*!"

Dysfunctional Home

For every troubled kid at school or other places, it is quite often possible to point at the underlying cracked foundation in their life: family. To say I had a dysfunctional home environment is the understatement of all lifetime. No one should have to put up with what I did growing up. By the time I reached eighth grade, I had attended fourteen different schools. My mother had married and divorced at least four times (and after I graduated from high school, she would add another divorce to her history). I'm not sure if my mother got married to her third husband or just lived with him. This unstable lifestyle did not make for a good foundation of my own views of marriage and commitment, and later in my life, it would play itself out by me repeating my mother's pattern in my first marriage.

I was talking to someone the other day and teaching him about finding value in yourself. My mother would go to bars and meet men, establish a relationship (all these men were alcoholics), marry them, and try to change them. Well, it never works and in the end; she would get a divorce and we would run, move, fourteen different schools in nine years.

Anyway, back to this person I was talking to. I told him a story about fishing. If you value yourself as a good catch, you will only expect the same. In other words, if you are desperate and you go fishing, you will catch and keep whatever you catch. So if you bring in a carp or a sucker fish, you'll keep it, thinking this is all your worth anyway; you're just happy to have a fish. If you find value in yourself, you will not keep the carp or sucker fish; you'll put them back and wait on a good catch, such as a bass or trout. Why, you find value in yourself and are not desperate! I don't know if my mother thought she was not valuable or if she thought she could fix these men; all I knew was she got married often, and we would run at some point.

When you live in a house that is not solidly founded in good family principles, everyone is joking for position, attention, and power, if you will. When I was in kindergarten, three of my four older brother and sisters came to live with us; they were from my mother's first marriage. They, too, had a tumultuous childhood and brought that chaos to the family. Then there was the violence, alcohol abuse, drug usage, and other insanity that left me fearful, confused, and often upset. All my siblings would tease me and one, a few years older than me (they were all older than me as I was the youngest), would beat the crap out of me until I got old enough to defend myself. This dysfunctional family left me with extreme anxiety and fear. I never knew when the onslaught of attacks would start and finish. They thought it was fun to watch me cry and freak out with anger. This anxiety carried over into my education. How was I supposed to concentrate on my studies with so much chaos in the house?

Yet what did I get from the educational system that is supposed to offer help and guidance to youngsters from such sad circumstances? Nothing, absolutely nothing. I'm not saying they were equipped to help with my home life, but they were educators and should have found a way to teach me or see that something was wrong. School could have been a sanctuary for me if they would only have taken the time to learn who I was as an individual and not labeled me wrongly. The schools stereotyping, ridicule, and outdated teaching methods that reflected how the teacher learned, not how I learned, keep me from progress. Everyone is capable of learning—but not everyone learns the same way. Any good teacher should understand this simple concept; they learn about learning when they attended college, or you would think they learned about how to teach, it's in their title! Are parents the people who instill the early foundation that is so crucial to a child's future, and who have continuing influence throughout their lives, be solely responsible for their child's education? We all know the answer to that; if your child attends a school, the educator has also taken on the responsibility to teach and educate the child. Whether a parent, a schoolteacher, or just someone who interacts with children, you must remember that you cannot classify or categorize a child until you have spent some time with him or her, discovering what type of issue or issues that child is dealing with. People who said I had a "learning disorder" would have a hard time explaining how I earned a bachelor's degree in business administration from TUI, a master's degree in ministry from Northwest University, and my second master's degree in leadership from Grand Canyon University, plus being an Army Ranger and Green Beret. Everyone who labeled me as moronic and classified me mentally disabled should be ashamed of themselves. They tore holes in my foundation before I could even get it established.

One of my problems originated with my premature birth while we were living in San Andreas, a small town in Northern California. Although the doctors didn't expect me to live, they had me flown two hours away to a hospital in San Francisco. That was my home for the next two years, at least, that's what my mother told me. My dad left home when I was seven, and we never had a decent relationship until I had reached the age of thirty. Years after the fact, when I asked him how long I had stayed at the hospital, he just said, "It was for a long time." My brother, who is twelve years older, and one of my older sisters collaborated with the long-time time stay in the hospital.

I used to question some of the stories my mother shared with me. After all, she told me I would not be athletic or engage in a lot of other physical activities. That would be news to anyone who watched me play football, run track, kickbox, or compete in tae kwon do. As a teenager, I placed third in the world championships for kickboxing, fighting men much older than me. I was also very active in the Northwest, competing in local karate tournaments and performing rather well, typically placing first in sparring and katas (a choreographed dance of movements in most martial arts). Later, I enlisted in the military and proved my abilities to handle tough physical and mental challenges, like the little selection process for Special Forces, haha. Anyone who has gone through Special Forces Selection knows is anything but little, easy. Considering what I had to endure growing up, it is a miracle I made it that far without being addicted to drugs and being in jail.

A Life of Mayhem

Several times, older guys molested me, starting in kindergarten (which I will discuss in another chapter.) I never knew the meaning of stability, whether that meant jumping around from temporary home to temporary home or enduring considerable chaos in our home. An older "sister" (actually, a girl my mother had informally adopted) used to beat the daylights out of me until I learned how to fight, and because of my ability to win the fights now, she stopped picking on me. I figure she must have been acting out some of her own frustrations that came from living amid constant arguing and fighting. Mom's first husband, the father of my older brothers and sisters, jacked them up regularly. He beat them with hoses or whatever else he could put his hands on. That is, if he wasn't using them to open a bottle. Even though my brothers and sisters are in their fifties and sixties, the scars from their childhood are still there. I often pray about this, wishing the scars could finally heal and we could act like a family.

Although my alcoholic father wasn't physically abusive to us kids, in his oft-drunken state, he regularly got into bar fights or arguments with Mom. I think Dad enjoyed fighting; many of his visits to the nearest tavern wound up degenerating into fist-swinging brawls. One time my oldest brother came running into the house yelling, "He's half-dead! He's half-dead! Dad is getting drowned by the Smith brothers!" A group of brothers Dad had irritated were taking his head, ramming it into a wall, and trying to drown him in a sink at the tavern. My oldest brother was there, drinking with him when the fight erupted. I still remember the panic and fright I felt witnessing the mayhem. All I could think of was Dad's head hitting the wall and the brothers holding his lifeless body up like a ragdoll while they shoved his face in the water. I'm not even sure how it ended; however, I know he survived to fight another day.

On another occasion, my brother's dog bit my sister (although it wasn't bad enough for her to see a doctor) while we were eating dinner. My father got so angry he suddenly grabbed a two-by-four with nails in it and beat the dog with it, blood spattering around the room. When I saw things like this, I froze with terror; I didn't know what to do. You might think that after I lived in this kind of chaos for such a long time, I would become accustomed to such a situation. That is not the case. Unless you are the aggressor, you're always scared. The time I clobbered that kid on the playground is one of the few occasions where I wasn't trying to hide or scared or dream that I could escape the insanity and live in a normal home.

I still remember the time in third grade when our next-door neighbors got in a huge brawl. I heard screams erupt—the kind that signals pain rather than fighting—and when I looked out the window, I saw this woman stabbing her husband with an ice pick. She stuck him in his head, shoulders, back, anywhere else she could stab him. His blood sprayed everywhere. Finally, he ran out the front of the house, around to the side, and disappeared out back, with his screaming wife in pursuit. Then both of them went back inside their house through the back door. During this melee, someone called the cops, who arrested her for stabbing her husband thirty-seven times. An ambulance carted him off to the hospital. I don't know what happened after that; I never saw them again.

Sometimes I got in fights myself. I still have a scar on my left hand from the time I smacked a kid in the mouth in grade school. I remember thinking, "I don't want to hit him with my right because I'll hurt him." So I whacked him with my left. I broke his tooth, but I wound up the loser—my hand got swollen and infected. Then, in eighth grade—soon after we had moved to another new place—the tough kids "called me out" and demanded I fight one of them. (Although I had only taken a few karate classes, I had bragged to classmates about having a black belt). I went out behind the video arcade building and squared off against one of the locals. I punched him in the face and knocked him down. After I let him get up, he lunged at me, and we went at it again. A wrestler, he tried taking me to the ground, but I didn't fall right away. However, when I tripped on a bush and wound up eating some leaves, he used a Heimlich maneuver on me. That ended the fight in his favor, but the bullies left me alone after that.

Constantly Provoked

I didn't just fight outside our home. As I mentioned, it was the girl who Mom took in out of pity and became like a sister who loved to pound on me whenever she got the chance. My siblings used to just verbally pick on me in an effort to provoke me and have a little fun. Although many people would think nothing of such harmless sibling horseplay because of all the other junk going on (being molested) in my life, it infuriated me. I felt like an eternal punching bag, and it shredded my heart. Sometimes, I wish it had just permanently hardened it. That might have made things a little easier on a young boy.

To make matters worse, since we were always moving I never developed any friendships or any sense of stability. Our family looked like pinballs as we moved from town to town and place to place. It was crazy, especially after Dad left (or Mom kicked him out, I'm not sure which) while I was a third-grader. One year, we lived in five different places. In kindergarten, I went to two different schools. Same for first grade, third, fourth, fifth, sixth, seventh, and eighth grade. Second grade almost felt like a dream, since I stayed in the same place all school year.

However, by third grade, I was yet another school, this time, a Christian-operated facility for the mentally or physically disabled. Actually, it wasn't that bad since we got to go to the YMCA every Friday for swimming class. Because I could swim, the teachers allowed me to swim in the deep end. I loved floating and bobbing up and down in the deep water. It felt fun, tranquil, and worry free. Although we didn't move that summer, when the next school year rolled around, I was at a different school. That is, until midway through the school year when we moved again.

The constant moving, coupled with sibling abuse and the chaos around me, took its toll. Periodically I would get so mad I would explode and do things to hurt myself. I would pound on walls until my hands bled. Sometimes I swung at loose boards, and if a nail happened to be sticking out, it was no big deal. On other occasions, I cut myself and let the blood squirt over my body. As strange as it may sound, this kind of physical pain relieved some of the pressure and pain I felt inside. When you hurt so badly on the inside, it seems preferable to hurt on the outside. I had to do something to get rid of the trauma, and I knew nobody would listen to me anyway. They never had.

Yet as bad as this all sounds, I never got mad at my mother. I felt sorry for her. She kept marrying alcoholics who were wildly unpredictable and undependable. Their addictions left them unable to fulfill their obligations as the man of the house or as a father figure to us kids. In fact, I credit my mother for the success I've enjoyed in life. She drilled it into my head that I could do anything I wanted. She continued to reinforce that I could do whatever I set my mind to. Even though I spell well and reading was a huge issue for me, she constantly reinforced I could do whatever I wanted. It may take me longer to learn it or I may have to work harder than everyone else, in the end, I was walking across that like everyone else. It proved to pay off; in the Army, I did well with my academic studies. Sometimes I did have to study harder and longer than most everyone else, but in the end, I was a Green Beret, just like everyone else.

With Mom's encouragement, I learned to work around my challenges. I saw that in life, everyone has strengths and weaknesses. Some people try to pretend they don't have any shortcomings, but I know better. Intelligent people capitalize on their strengths and find others who can help them in their weak areas. No CEO running a large corporation knows everything about everything and how to do everything. He or she hires capable people and turns them loose to do their job. That is what makes good leaders: people wise enough to recognize what they don't know and find someone who does know and has the skills needed.

My experience in rising above the horrible circumstances of my childhood, this is one reason I react so strongly to those who categorize or put down children. Kids of all ages believe about anything an adult tells them. I still remember the high school English teacher who told me, "You'll never amount to anything. When you graduate, you should go get a job digging ditches. That's about all you'll be able to accomplish." Excuse me? How did she know that? She didn't! She saw a moment in time where I struggled with reading and spelling, not knowing about the molestation or broken homes or nomadic lifestyle that I had endured for most of my life. It wasn't because I was dumb; it was because I had a poor education.

Family

Turnaround Comes

While it took a long time, I started to make a turnaround my freshman year of high school. No sooner had the fall term started, my mother declared her intentions to move yet again. I had enough. I refused, telling her, "I'm not going. This has to stop. I'll move in with Brad" (my best friend then; I still consider him a buddy, even though we haven't seen each other for a while). My declaration persuaded her to scrap the idea. After years of chaos, by now she ran a restaurant in a neighboring town called the Cozy Corner Café, and it started paying off. By high school, we weren't so poor. I remember, for many years, how we used to make toast. If we left the bread in the toaster too long, we just had to scrape the burn off before eating it.

After craving stability for years, I finally gained some. Not only did I start making friends; we weren't constantly pulling up stakes, my athletic skills gave me some confidence. It wasn't that I was a good athlete; it was because in the past, every time we moved somewhere new, I would have to prove myself all over again. Fortunately, in the town where we lived, they didn't have organized youth football for kids below eighth grade, so I didn't have to compete against a wealth of experienced players.

My speed and jumping ability also came in handy in track. I liked the chance to excel and stand out in individual competitions. You're either fast or you're not. You either jump far or you don't. Added to the acclaim I earned for my track and football skills was the long-awaited sense of stability I finally felt. Staying in the same place all four years of high school was like a dream come true.

Still, although my fortunes were looking up, I still had to deal with the guilt of my past. Not just the sexual incidents. I remember getting drunk as a third grader, and in fifth grade, one of my brothers introduced me to marijuana. Then there was the fear that lurked in the shadows, leaving me feeling confused and upset. I never felt unloved or unwanted. Yet the unspoken questions still swirled in my mind: "Why are you guys treating me like crap? Why can't you act decently like some of the guys I know? What did I do wrong?" Of course, my siblings weren't necessarily at fault. Their lives were more jacked up than mine.

The thing that so many people from a middle or upper-class background don't understand is how many children from impoverished families, or ones ripped apart by alcoholism or drug addiction, are just scraping by. They face a daily struggle to survive. The people who should be their role models and help them build a foundation are a mess themselves. You can look down your nose at kids like that and think, "How disgusting," but those who do that have likely never dealt with dysfunctional lifestyles.

When you're poor, if a parent, neighbor, or friend steals something and you benefit from that, you don't feel any guilt. After all, things are better now than they were before. The victim doesn't enter your thoughts or you rationalize: "Well, they probably stole it from someone else. So I've got something now. Hey, this is good." If the adults around you are stealing, drinking, or getting high all the time, what are you going to think is normal? When everyone around is drinking and smoking dope, you won't see that as wrong. Everybody else in your family is doing it. What's the big deal?

When Colorado and Washington decided to legalize pot in 2014, I don't think they realize what a Pandora's Box they opened up. When I visited Seattle right before the state finalized its regulations regarding sales, I could smell a sickening sweet odor walking up the steps from the waterfront because some dude was out smoking it openly. How many kids will that one guy impact negatively in years to come? Then multiply that by a million. The month before Washington issued the first group of twenty licenses for marijuana retail stores, the governor announced a campaign to make sure pot stayed out of the hands of minors. Yeah, right. That will work about as well as the liquor laws. Once again, adults made decisions with no regard for what kind of foundation they were laying for society's most powerless, impressionable members.

CHAPTER 2
The Foundation of the Apple Tree

In chapter 1, you read about some of the chaotic events of my childhood, including getting sexually molested in kindergarten, getting drunk for the first time in first grade, and getting high with my brother as a third-grader. Since Mom could never find a man that she could stay with, by eighth grade, I had attended fourteen different schools. Even though she failed at marriage, my mother succeeded at parenting. She constantly told me that I was a wonderful child with value and could accomplish anything I set my mind to do. That helped counteract the cruel teachers and school officials who branded me mentally retarded and proclaimed I would never amount to anything.

However, many people can't overcome the rotten foundation they receive in childhood. Life is like an apple tree. To raise a fruitful apple tree, the first thing growers must do is prepare the ground to receive the seed. They must choose the right time for planting, take special precautions digging the hole, put the right nutrients into it, and cover it up with the right amount of dirt. They must nurture the seed and water the ground before the seed will blossom into a healthy apple tree. So it is with life. The foundation of our growth starts with our parents and relies greatly on the values and teaching they learned from their parents.

In the aftermath of wars in Vietnam and the Middle East wars in recent decades, we have heard much about post-traumatic stress disorder or PTSD. This ailment can stem from tragedies other than war, too, be that a serious accident, domestic violence, or sexual abuse. However, 75 to 80 percent of adults overcome the problem with various coping strategies. In other words, they learn to live with it. They are like an apple tree with a lemon branch grafted in. At some point, they cut off the foreign branch and move on with life.

Yet when children are subjected to intense anguish and pain, those qualities are grafted into their root system. That adds extra hurt and trauma to their lives. When their tree matures, its blossoms bear the fruit of strange and unfamiliar things that shaped them. While millions of people overcome such trauma as their parents' divorce, death, physical abuse, sexual abuse, or mental abuse, the pain hasn't necessarily vanished. As they grow into adults, they still have this nagging element in their root system. Ridding themselves of it is not a simple challenge; sometimes it is nearly impossible. This is why it is imperative that we adults lay that good foundation for our children, even if we struggled with the impact of a faulty foundation.

The Effects of Trauma

In overcoming my past, and in mentoring and counseling numerous people over the years, I have seen the mighty struggles posed by childhood trauma. A current example is the young man I have been counseling who can't overcome the pain of his past, even though he was adopted by an American family at the age of eight. As a three-year-old boy, his mother—who couldn't afford to raise him—gave him away to another woman. In his native country, children lack value, as seen by what happened next. Although his foster mother raised him for the next few years, she then met a man. He didn't like the boy and gave her the ultimatum: "It's him or me." She decided she wanted to stay with this man, so she abandoned him on the streets.

He ran the streets for a while begging, stealing, and doing whatever it took to get food and survive. Finally, one day, some authorities picked him up and placed him in a foster home.

That may sound like a reasonable solution, but the foster home where he landed was barely a cut above the streets. When finally adopted by an American family, it seemed like a dream come true. However, the seed of rejection planted so long ago meant he grew into a young man with a slew of problems. Despite a much better environment, questions nagged at his mind: How long will this family actually keep me? Will they give me away too? What dangers will I face later?

Try as they did, his new family couldn't adequately prune his damaged root system. He fell into problems that threatened to send him off to juvenile hall. Finally, he stopped stealing, but continued to mistrust everyone. Even though he graduated from high school, years later, he doesn't have a healthy relationship with his adoptive parents. Nor does he have good relationships with peers and co-workers. Now in his early thirties, he still has issues with trust. I have worked with him for two years, trying to repair his foundation and a root system laden with loneliness, bitterness, untrustworthiness, and low self-esteem.

A toddler left on the streets to fend for himself is just one example of a battered family structure and the faulty foundation that has been laid in countless numbers of lives. The root system planted in him should have produced a delicious red apple. Instead, it yielded corrupted, tainted, bitter, sour fruit. No one wants to eat of it. Not surprisingly, it has taken considerable time, patience, painstaking effort, and love to show him that I will do whatever it takes to help him.

One of the lessons I have regularly reviewed with him is about the apple tree and how his is producing sour fruit instead of the sweet and delicious kind. It took about eighteen months before he started to understand the sour fruit he was producing was not his fault; it sprouted from seeds planted years before. Now all he can do is move forward. Although I wondered if we would reach that point, he finally started to trust me. At one time, he looked at himself as if he had no future or hope. This has started to change.

Chances are, you know someone who came from a background of dysfunction and deprivation, even if not this extreme. Considering how many people there are in our society whose lives have been marred by drugs, alcohol, abuse, or other chaos, stemming the tide may appear hopeless. Yet none of us is called to save the world. We just need to help the person in front of us. We may not be able to help everybody, but we can help one person. In turn, that person may reach out in the future and help someone else. Turnarounds come one step at a time.

Early Lessons

I like the illustration of an apple tree because it offers such a perfect parallel to the human body. Just like a tender apple shoot, as babies, people need the most nurturing and care. Yet just as the tree craves nourishment, infant children are like sponges, soaking up everything around them—good or bad. Recently my wife, Teresa, and I were out shopping when a little girl who looked to be about five years old grabbed a toy off one of the shelves and said, "I've crushed my 'nuts.'" Obviously, she had heard her father or someone else in her family make this kind of remark. She equated it with something that must be funny because it probably sparked laughter at home. I know that's a simple example, but it illustrates how everything we do as parents or influencers of children helps build the foundation of their root system.

Whether children learn crude remarks, sarcasm, and emotional explosions, or more positive traits like thoughtfulness, kindness, and generosity, their future actions stem from the root system developed at a young age. When children throw tantrums, are rebellious, or otherwise "act out," we may wonder where they learned such boorish behavior. Not on their own, for sure. To expect them to automatically change when they grow older is unrealistic.

Our relationships with our family, whether parents, siblings, or extended family members, have a considerable impact on our root system. But so does our economic status, education, spiritual beliefs, and especially culture—the beliefs, customs, attitudes, and outlook of a particular group. That can apply to our family background, the organization where we work, or other spheres in which we operate. Culture definitely dictates the way we think, how we perceive the world, expectations of the future, how we treat others, and the values we embrace. So if someone lives in an upper middle-class neighborhood, both parents have a college degree, and both parents work, this micro-culture demonstrates to their children values of education, a work ethic, and their expectations and economic status.

However, someone like me, who grew up in a single-parent household and never sees the role model of a dependable stepfather, is going to be affected by this micro-culture as well. Naturally, I came into my first marriage with a skewed image of marriage. If things didn't work out, I thought you could just throw away that spouse and start over. A divorce and other factors helped me realize I had to reform the way I looked at marriage if I hoped to succeed at it.

Another trait that emerged from my micro-culture is my ability to make friends. That quality emerged from necessity. Since Mom had this special ability to link up with alcoholics who declined her encouragement to stop drinking, I grew up in a constantly-disrupted home. Moving from place to place regularly and enrolling in a string of new schools meant I had a horrible educational foundation. Today, I don't particularly like moving (though my Army career moved me all over the United States.) However, because we moved so much, I learned to make friends easily.

Long-Lasting Impact

Many people fail to recognize how seriously their foundation impacts their lives. Recently, a friend told me about counseling a man in his twenties who had already been married twice. While doing some marriage counseling, my friend learned that this young man had grown up with a verbally-abusive mother. She treated his father with little respect and ran the house like an iron-willed dictator. Naturally, this young man vowed to never allow this to happen to him. As a result, in every romantic relationship he found himself in, he acted disrespectfully and sought to control his significant other, acting like his dictatorial mother. Because of his root system, he struggled in every relationship, his previous marriage, and his current marriage. Though this young man had a number of options, he only saw two—he could either let the women in his life be like his mom and rule and dictate over him, or not let that happen.

This is what often happens when we grow up with a flawed root system. Whether veering to the right or the left, we go to extremes. For example, somebody who grows up poor vows to never be poor again, so they do whatever it takes to be wealthy—at all costs, even if they wind up ruining their marriage and home life because of their irrational fear of becoming poor again. Others shrug their shoulders, sit down, and let someone else take care of them. They remain in the same state in which they were raised.

Many young men who grow up in fatherless homes live in neighborhoods that reflect their family culture. Seeking what they're missing—respect, admiration, and fatherly love—they go looking for other men they can look up to and say, "This man is strong." It isn't surprising so many wind up in gangs and a culture of violence and corruption. If not redirected, this foundation will bear rotten fruit for a lifetime. I see this in a friend who was part of the Mexican Mafia in Los Angeles thirty years ago. Although incarcerated as a teenager and as a young adult, today is he is a prison minister. Yet he still looks like a gangster. His clothes, his speech, and even his mustache reflect the foundation laid in his childhood.

In the same way this ex-Mafioso struggles with his past, so do the students of a friend who teaches high school. Many of her students come from impoverished circumstances. With a foundation laid in poverty, they don't see the value of education. Nor do they believe that they will ever have a high-paying job or own their own home. Because they see no future and believe that there will ultimately wind up in the same situation as their parents, they don't try to do anything that could lift them out of despair and change their situation. My friend continually emphasizes the value of education and not from an elitist viewpoint of just promoting a college degree. She stresses the value of skills they could acquire with vocational training so they can develop marketable skills. She advises them, "When you graduate from high school, you can have the skills that other people want and will pay you to use."

She also talks about ways to obtain grants, or low-interest loans, and internships that can help them acquire valuable knowledge as she tries to instill values in them. Too often it's like talking to a brick wall. With their foundation laid in hopelessness, they don't believe this can happen for them. All around them, they see plenty of evidence: poor role models, deadbeat dads, violence in their neighborhoods, and 90 percent of other students on subsidized lunch plans. Too many parents fail to appreciate that, even if they live in modest circumstances, they can improve their children's future through training and encouragement. They don't grasp that if they nurture those young apple trees, they can blossom later in life. That's what my mother did. We didn't live like kings, but I grew up believing I could live better. And I do.

Value of Education

These defeatist attitudes that come from those in poverty are sad because education is such a key area when it comes to overcoming poverty. More parents need to value an education. When I grew up, I heard a litany of grumbling, complaining, and negative comments about schools. People would say things like, "Why do you need to go to college? It just costs money to do something that you can already do." To that, I would say that education doesn't necessarily mean college. There are numerous other means of education that help provide marketable skills that produce an income for you and your family.

Recently I went to a funeral. I happened to arrive a bit early and had some time to chat with the funeral home's director. I asked him how he had gotten into the business. He told me in high school he took an aptitude test, and it said he should go into preaching, politics, or (no kidding) become a funeral director. He said he didn't want to be a preacher, nor did he want to go into politics. So he chose funeral director and sat down with a guidance counselor to map out a plan. Because he found a marketable skill that people were willing to pay for, he has never been unemployed. Forty years later, he's still working and owns his own business.

Granted, he started with not much money and for many years had to work for others. However, about ten years ago, he purchased his first funeral home and now owns three. Now, the average person may look at his choice as a bit morbid, but sooner or later, everyone needs funeral services. Since his parents instilled a foundation in him and promoted the importance of education and acquiring a marketable skill, he grew up and flourished instead of withering away. While it took a lot of hard work, those seeds took root and established long-lasting fruit.

Strong Root System

That funeral director demonstrates the value of family when it comes to a strong root system. Not just parents, but brothers and sisters, aunts and uncles, cousins, grandparents, and friends. This is where seeds get planted and apple trees are nurtured. Yet as my life shows, childhood trauma is no excuse to just throw up your hands and quit. Yes, it will affect you for the rest of your life, but a perfect home environment doesn't guarantee a perfect outcome either. Ever know someone who grew up in a middle- or upper-class home and yet wound up as a drug addict or criminal? Or someone who grew up dirt poor and was a gang member, but turned his life around and now works as a doctor, lawyer, or business owner?

What these stories show is the power of individual choices. Yes, it is tough for the average person to overcome a poor foundation. When things get entrenched in a young life, it can be a monumental challenge to pull away from them. And yet, it isn't impossible. One reason is that our development doesn't stop in childhood. The human brain continues to grow and learn into our twenties, and we can continue learning well beyond young adulthood.

Sometimes in life, we simply have to start over. We can't allow a bad root system, one laden with a corruptible seed, to go on and bear rotten, sour fruit. Go through your past and find the best seed that you can. Stop dwelling on all the negatives and accentuate the positives. Nurture and care for yourself and grow into something beautiful. It is never too late to start over, or set a good example for another and help lay a good foundation for them. It is never too late to plant a tree. Many negative voices around you may declare it's too late. It's not. People that have been physically abused, sexually abused, mentally abused, classified as mentally handicapped, and who grew up scraping burnt off their toast because they were so poor, do not have to accept that as their foundation. They can produce good fruit if they try. I know this to be true because all the things that happened to me.

As I continued to grow and mature into adulthood, I decided I didn't want to be those things that others had declared about my future. I vowed that I could do more than what my root system had laid in me. If your foundation was screwed up from the beginning like mine, or that young adult I have been counseling, it does not mean you have to accept your past as your identity or an indelible mark of your future. As someone who was unable to read until I reached eighth grade, regularly suffered ridicule and put-downs from both my peers and teachers, I know what it's like to have that negative chorus ringing in your ears.

Maybe you know what it's like to hear those voices. Maybe there is little in your life growing up that was positive. Still, that doesn't mean that you have to accept that as your lot in life. Prune your tree, establish a new foundation, and create a new, positive voice. So what if you have to start late in life? So what if you have to start over? It's not where you've been but where you're going that will make a difference in your life. Find others who are positive and can help motivate you. Find something that will inspire you to get you to where you want to be and who you want to become. Do not make excuses and tell yourself that you don't know anyone who can help you. If necessary, make some new friends. Find a new mentor. Associate with those who can encourage you in your dreams. If you want to become a professional basketball player, you shouldn't hang out with golfers. If you want to be successful in life—whatever that definition is for you—find those type of people and create a new foundation. Plant a new tree.

My mother always told me that I may have to study harder, but so what? No matter how hard I had to study, or how many hours I had to work while others were out playing basketball, in the end, I would walk across that stage the same as the rest of them. And that is just what happened.

CHAPTER 3

The Foundation of Learning

Although I don't think anything ranks higher in establishing a solid (or faulty) foundation in a child's life than family, helping children learn life skills in addition to such basics as reading, math, and science is another essential component of that foundation. It is also relevant to every person reading these words. After all, every one of us is a teacher. If you are a parent, you are teaching your children every day. If you are a teacher in a classroom setting, you are playing a vital role in teaching other people's children. However, those are only two of the more obvious. If you are the CEO of a company, a manager, a supervisor, or even a brother, sister, aunt, or uncle you are—or will be—teaching someone. Everyone teaches others. Leaders are teaching all the time, whether it is called mentoring, leading, or a conference.

Have you ever wondered why some people *get it* and others *don't*? As I learned from my struggles in learning to read and spell, this often reflects on the teacher's ability. Throughout elementary school and into the years that followed, most of my teachers could never recognize my learning style. They wanted to teach me various subjects, particularly reading, in the same way they had learned them earlier in their lives. Yet their learning style didn't match mine. Ironically, I would go on to spend the majority of my life teaching, starting with the tae kwon do school I owned and operated while still in high school.

After high school, when I enlisted in the United States Army, I taught all the time—especially during my years as a Green Beret. In a short span of time, I saw that teaching others with the same method as I learned a subject is not effective. In the army, the meaning of teaching takes on a whole new importance. My ability to teach well literally spelled the difference between life and death. When my survival depended on how well I taught and how well my students learned, it made identifying various learning styles of utmost importance. When a week later (or a month or some other brief time frame) the troops I instructed might attract enemy fire, I realized I needed to grasp how my students learned instead of focusing on my preferences.

I break down teaching into four styles. The first is auditory; auditory learners learn from hearing the material. Think of the common lecture style of imparting knowledge. The second way is kinesthetic. These types of learners grasp lessons through touching or doing. A person with a kinesthetic bent learns from a "hands-on" approach. What's more, they often get quite frustrated with teachers who want them to learn in some other way. The next type is the visual learner. This is the type of person who needs a demonstrative, "show me how it's done" kind of instruction. The fourth type is often classified as visual as well, but my experience says otherwise. This is the intellectual, engineer type. Such a person learns best by reading. He or she prefers to read the information as opposed to sitting or going through (for them) the grinding punishment of a visual, hands-on approach. If forced to sit through a demonstration, the intellectual thinks, *I understand. Why do we have to do this? I can read the manual.*

Overcoming Barriers

However, there is also a fifth style: the combination of the four primary ones. As a Green Beret, I taught all over the world, meaning I frequently dealt with language barriers. (I didn't just work with military enlistees; my career included working with such agencies as the Special Air Service, the French Foreign Legion, and US border patrol units.) Although I worked with translators, any time my language got translated into another tongue, confusion could arise. Whether because a slight mistake by the translator or the fact there weren't words or terms in the other language that directly paralleled English, things didn't always translate in a neat package. Besides the language barrier, even if my students spoke English there were often regional differences or cultural idioms to overcome.

One of our duties as Green Berets—or Special Forces as they are known throughout the four branches of the military—involved training soldiers from other nations to defend themselves. We helped transform indigenous armies into cohesive fighting units. That could mean guerilla warfare in one place, people opposing an oppressive regime in another, or helping a government seeking to turn back terrorists.

One time we were summoned to Tonga, an island in the South Pacific populated by Polynesians, a people similar to Samoans and Hawaiians. This was rugged, survivalist-type training where we used real bullets. While they spoke English, the cultural gaps were huge. Tonga is a monarchy ruled by a king, where the rules and expectations are miles apart from American customs. The various differences meant we had to be careful how we phrased our language and terms. In addition, it is a very macho society. Although our engineer and demolition guy stood six-foot-three and weighed 240 pounds, they focused more attention on our medic. Although he packed 180 pounds of solid muscle on his six-foot frame, they called him "a little white guy." (Since I only stood five-foot-nine, I'm not sure what they called me.)

After one week into our three-week mission, we were about to lose our minds. These guys weren't listening very closely. Sometimes it seemed like we were talking to a brick wall. Finally, one day in frustration, I grabbed the platoon sergeant and flung him to the ground. Standing over him, I screamed, "Look, you dummies! The urgency of this is life and death, and if you're not going to listen, I'm going to leave!" The silence was deafening. After the sergeant picked himself up and nodded at his troops, everything changed. Since I had just proved myself a man, for the rest of our stay, they listened to everything we said and carried out our tactical training orders. We never again had to tell them twice. But in this macho environment, they weren't going to listen until I showed them I could be a tough guy too.

In terms of overcoming language barriers, that proved toughest with troops from Nepal, Bangladesh, and Middle Eastern countries. These were infantry units, equivalent to our US Army infantry units by duty and responsibility. The thing that frustrated me the most was trying to teach foreign soldiers to "zero" a weapon. Essentially, that means to look down the sight of a gun so you can determine where the crosshairs align so you can better hit the target. Trying to find a way to phrase that in a way translators could transmit this information proved to be a formidable challenge in many places. Sometimes I could get translator to properly tell them how to zero a weapon one day, but the next day they might say something different. To this day, I wonder why it was such a battle to get this concept across.

Lifelong Instructors

As I mentioned, I started teaching in high school in my own tae kwon do school, which many would call karate. At the time, I didn't even realize how I incorporated four learning styles into my classes.

- The first was visual: I demonstrated a particular technique or had another instructor or expert student to demonstrate it for me.
- Next I communicated the importance of doing a particular move or

set of moves in the prescribed manner. This isn't just a key in martial arts. No matter what the subject, students need to know the *why* behind the *what* of their lessons. I remember numerous students asking a question like, "I want to be a mechanic. Why do I need to learn calculus?" and never get an answer. If someone doesn't know *why* they need to learn something, I can guarantee they won't apply themselves to learning the subject.
- Then I would have students execute the move, which would be the kinesthetic, action-type learning.
- For the person who was analytical, I had to explain it to them so it made sense to them.

I went around the class and picked out students by the way they seemed to learn the best. Then, during individual instruction time, I tried to maximize their potential by using that style.

We had a wide range of students, from the age of eight to folks in their fifties. One young guy was a genius; he earned a black belt at eleven and made the national rankings a year or two later. Since he was so analytical, I had to explain a lot of things to him. But once he understood it, he could do it well. With other students, I would have to tell them repeatedly and sometimes show them several times as well. Not surprisingly, he later earned his master's degree and is now an electrical engineer.

While many reading this may have no military or martial arts experience, the application of this principle still applies to your life: Whoever you are teaching, you must use a multifaceted approach. You can adapt once you learn an individual's style, but in a larger setting, you must teach all ways because you won't know how all the students learn best. Your goal is to make sure they understand the material, learn the material—and most importantly —can execute what they have learned.

This is a lifelong process. If you are a parent, your job isn't simply to put a roof over your children's heads, food on the table, and clothes on their back. You must maintain a constant awareness of what you are teaching them while understanding how they learn. You are the teacher and they are the learners; it is your job to teach them so they learn their lessons well. One child is likely to learn differently than his or her other siblings, and in a different style than you did as a child. Once you identify each child's style, you will become a much more effective teacher. And, as older parents can assure you, you will be teaching them long after they leave home to establish their independence.

There are definite rewards to mastering your children's learning style and then teaching them in that manner. Once children discover they can learn, they become highly motivated to learn more. Since your children's teachers only have a brief moment in time to determine the styles of their two or three dozen students, parents can be of great help by informing their instructors how your child learns. This doesn't mean all teachers will listen, so when your kids have homework, teach them the way they learn, not necessarily the way the teacher insists they learn.

I wish I had had a parent emphasizing my learning style with my teachers. Perhaps more of them would have avoided labeling me as "slow" or "handicapped." Such putdowns infuriated me. I knew I wasn't a dummy, but I couldn't learn the way the teachers wanted to teach. Teachers should never label kids who came from circumstances like mine. Most have no grasp of a child's often-chaotic home environment.

Not only do they use more than one style, good teachers encourage their students to set high goals. In the military, I wanted to become a Delta Force operator. These soldiers were the equivalent of the Seal Team 6 guys who hunted down and killed Osama Bin Laden—the "all pros" of the Army. Since Delta Force represented the best of the best, I decided that was the level I wanted to achieve. I still remember the staff sergeant who led my sniper squad in the Army. He used to tell us, "Any time you go to military school, go to be number one. If you don't make number one, you graduate. If you go just to graduate, you may not graduate. When you are in the Army, Sunday evening through Thursday evening belongs to the Army. So study. Friday night and Saturday night is your time, so go have a good time. If you do that, you'll do well."

I took his advice to heart and followed it throughout my military career; I still apply it today. Because of what he taught me, I did very well in all the military schools I attended, graduating at the top of most of my classes. I am fortunate to have been one of his students; he was very influential in my career. He understood the concept of learning the learner's style better than most and his leadership carried me through the rest of my military career. I got promoted faster than most and retired as a master sergeant. While that is not at the top of the enlisted ranks, because of various circumstances, I did not compete for sergeant major's rank and chose to retire from the Army.

Setting a Foundation

Although I am convinced I would have been selected as a Delta Force operator, I chose not to try out or go to their selection because life changed dramatically when my children arrived (followed by an unfortunate divorce). While I did not reach Delta Force, I did become a Green Beret, which in my book is still a great accomplishment. So by setting a high goal, I wound up as a Green Beret, an Army Ranger, and a sniper. In other words, I accomplished a lot just by aiming high. The same is true with kids in high school. If they say "I can't go to college," they won't. Parents, why not tell your kids they can go to college? Why not assure them that they can get their Masters' degree? What's the worst that might happen? That they fizzle out and only wind up with a few college credits? So what? Consider the alternatives. Once they get there, they may successfully adapt and decide, "Hey, I can do this."

So what if your child is not college material and isn't cut out for life on campus? Remember college is not the only way to get educated. It isn't even suited for a guy who wants to study auto mechanics or truck driving school to earn a commercial driver's license. (And for those who turn up their nose at driving a truck, people with experience and a CDL can make $50,000 a year.) Whatever the choice, setting your target too low is a prescription for remaining on the bottom rungs of the career ladder. As an example, my brother-in-law works for the railroad as a laborer. He realized if he wants to be competitive for advancement and the chance to move to the management level, he needed to further his education. So he enrolled in college and is studying business management with an emphasis in human behavior.

When it comes to the power of encouragement, one of my favorite examples is the Jewish people. Although making up just two-tenths of 1 percent of the world's population, they represent 54 percent of the world chess champions, 27 percent of the Nobel physics laureates, and 31 percent of the medicine laureates. While only 2 percent of the United States' population, they make up 21 percent of Ivy League students, 26 percent of Kennedy Center honorees, 37 percent of Academy Award winning directors, and 51 percent of the Pulitzer Prize winners for nonfiction. *New York Times* columnist David Brooks cited those statistics in a 2010 column in which he mentioned how Steven L. Pease, author of *The Golden Age of Jewish Achievement*, lists some of the explanations people have given for this record of achievement.

"The Jewish faith encourages a belief in progress and personal accountability," Brooks writes. "It is learning-based, not rite-based. Most Jews gave up or were forced to give up farming in the Middle Ages; their descendants have been living off of their wits ever since. They have often migrated, with a migrant's ambition and drive. They have congregated around global crossroads and have benefited from the creative tension endemic in such places. No single explanation can account for the record of Jewish achievement. The odd thing is that Israel has not traditionally been strongest where the Jews in the Diaspora were strongest. Instead of research and commerce, Israelis were forced to devote their energies to fighting and politics."[1]

While I am not a noted scholar, I see the seeds of the Jews' greatness in the way they are raised. They are more accomplished than any other segment of society because parents encourage their children to be wise in the way they manage money, learn all they can, and to aim high. From early childhood, many Jewish children learn the "jar system." Parents give them four jars and ten dollars. They teach them that one dollar goes into a jar for God, another for savings, and another dollar for future educational or other expenses. Then they can live on the remaining seven dollars. By raising their children with expectations and teaching them to be creative and dynamic, parents often create a self-fulfilling prophecy.

On the other hand, I have seen the downside of low expectations. My wife is of Hispanic descent, an educator; she laments how many of her students aim for nothing more than a life of manual labor and minimum wage jobs. If you want to see your children rise above low-paying jobs or minimum-wage position, you must encourage them to aim higher. For example, our area is heavy in agriculture. If your child is showing interest in agriculture, encourage him or her to be trained in becoming a foreman (the boss) or better yet, become the owner of their own farm. You may have low expectations for yourself, or think it is too late for you to rise any higher, but don't instill your limitations on your children.

The Encouragement Lifeline

Encouragement is crucial to a child's future. I mentioned in chapter 1 how little encouragement my teachers provided for me. It started early in life when my lack of reading ability became apparent to teachers as well as my classmates. It wasn't just the belittling and ridicule aimed in my direction that hurt; it was the lack of caring. That message came through as loudly as if the teachers had broadcasted it through a megaphone. One time in my seventh-grade geography class, I accidentally dropped a pencil. It landed point up, with its violent rebound driving the pencil into my hand. When I went to show the teacher the blood dripping from my hand to show him I needed help, he spat, "Go sit down. I can take care of that after school."

About halfway through that school year, Mom moved us again. If I thought things would get better because I was in a new middle school, I was sadly mistaken. Even though by now I could read, I still couldn't do it too well. One teacher seemingly liked to call on me to read out loud so he could watch me squirm. Whenever he did, I would get so nervous that instead of seeing words on a page, they all meshed into an indecipherable mess. In terror of getting embarrassed and ridiculed, I would barely get out, "The... boy... jumped... over... the... before the laughter and hooting began.

This kind of stuff continued in high school. I remember the high school science teacher who constantly belittled me in class. I still hated reading out loud, something that it didn't take a genius to appreciate. This guy would degrade my learning abilities by making little snide remarks or comments addressed to me. When he called on me to read aloud, he would say things like, "Uh-oh, it's Mr. Walsh's turn to read again. Oh well, we'll see how he does. I certainly hope we'll get through this lesson before the end of class." Because of the fear of physical punishment crossing the line and turning into child abuse, many school systems have outlawed corporal punishment. I wonder how many limit verbal abuse.

Despite my struggles, I graduated from high school. Thanks to my athletic skills, I also got to see the world, traveling to China once for a competition sponsored by the International Sports Exchange. I competed in the long jump and triple jump. For a kid from such a dysfunctional background, even being there felt like stepping into a dream come true. In general, athletics gave me a foot up on my shortcomings. Although only five-foot-nine, I could slam dunk a basketball, although I never played outside of pick-up games on the playground. My junior year in football, I played running back and free safety. I led our team in rushing, passing, receiving, and interceptions, and rated second in tackles. I even ran back kickoffs and received several football scholarship offers and a couple in track.

Instead of a straight line to college, though, I waited until I had completed seventeen years of military service to attend Trident University International, a military-oriented school just south of Los Angeles. They had an SOC program, which stands for Service Opportunity Colleges. Although there weren't that many at first, the military now has 1,700 SOC schools nationwide. SOCs are set up so students can attend one campus, and when the military transfers them to another base close to an SOC school, they can enroll there without losing any credits. Fortunately, I didn't have to exercise that option and earned my bachelor's degree in business.

A Crucial Role

So why do I share all this? To let teachers and parents know what a crucial role you play in establishing a child's foundation. These are impressionable lives you are helping to shape. Label someone a "no-good loser," and he may grow up to become a self-fulfilling prophecy. Tell a young girl she's "a tramp" and she may wind up out on the streets ten or fifteen years later. Don't label youngsters who have their whole life ahead of them. Don't make them think they aren't any good and don't stand a chance. Who made you a prophet?

Remember, a good teacher is adaptable. Too many teachers say, "This is it's done. This is the way I was taught. This is the way I learned the best. That's the way I want to do it." That's wrong. As a person, you need to understand children don't come out of a cookie cutter. If you are a parent and your children are struggling in school, it may be because no one has taken the time to understand how they learn. If you will take time to talk with them, observe them closely, and see what lights up their eyes, you may discover how they learn.

When it comes to a child's self-esteem, anyone can go overboard and praise everything a child does, even when he or she puts forth a half-hearted effort. Or when their actions are wrong and what the child needs is a healthy dose of correction. More often than not, though, the problem is the world inflicting a sour-faced, negative outlook on kids and making them everything stinks before they have had a chance to discover life.

Bless those parents who look at a child and say, "Oh, man, I believe you can do anything." I've known parents who don't want to give their kids any positive feedback for fear they will develop overly-generous self-esteem. If that describes you, remember you need to promote your children. You need to tell them they can accomplish anything they set their mind to do. If you try to build them up and they don't quite make it, they are still further along than where they started. With your support and enthusiasm, they may develop the courage to try until they experience a breakthrough.

Notes

1. David Brooks, "The Tel Aviv Cluster," *New York Times*, January 11, 2010, http://www.nytimes.com/2010/01/12/opinion/12brooks.html?_r=0.

CHAPTER 4

The Foundation of Intimacy

Intimacy. The complete sharing of yourself with another person. This is designed as a gift exclusively for your spouse, stemming from the feelings of love and affection developed gradually over time. This foundation is essential for a happy life. However, with our modern, casual attitude that separates sex from love, I fear as a society we are wrecking too many children's futures before they can unfold. There are so many types and forms of liaisons projected as normal and natural that in American society confusion reigns supreme.

In my case, it is only by the grace of God that I didn't wind up incredibly warped. My first exposure to sexual molestation came in kindergarten. At least, that's when I remember it taking place; I can only remember bits and pieces of childhood prior to the age of seven. Psychologists would say my mind blocked out many of the memories because they are so unpleasant. I wouldn't disagree with such an observation. Indeed, I consider my inability to remember much of this trauma a blessing.

Unfortunately, I remember enough of what happened to describe the basics. The molester was a teenager, the son of some friends of my parents. My parents liked to by stop their home every week or two. These people lived then on a country road on an Indian reservation in the state of Washington. A paved highway ran in front of the house where they lived, but the side road was dirt. On the dirt side sat a tree house that someone had built up in a tree where most of the branches had been removed. We often went to play in that tree house when the molester proposed we go outside and my dad agreed, telling me, "Go outside and play." Back in the 1970s, there were no video games, smart phones, or cable networks with five hundred options. Even when I protested that I didn't want to go, the molester kept suggesting it until I gave in and went outside. Although at first I had fun played different games and chatting, I later realized how cleverly this guy was grooming me.

Looking back with the benefit of years of service in Special Forces, I can see how he used the same tactics we did when we trained other soldiers to go into battle. When we first went into another country, we couldn't expect people to automatically go out and accept the violence that accompanies enemy warfare. We had to first develop rapport and friendship. Once they called us "friend," they started trusting in us, which allowed us to influence them. The same is true of a new teacher. If she comes walking into a class and the first thing she says is, "On Friday we'll have a test," the kids are likely to scratch their heads and wonder, *Who are you? We don't even know you.* The teacher has to be able to develop a relationship with students so they trust her (or him). Then she can influence them.

This is what somebody does when they want to manipulate you. This guy was a master and enjoyed numerous opportunities to beguile my young mind. At first when we went outside, he would ask, "What do you want to play?" So we played different games. After another few visits, he suggested going up to the playhouse. After we had climbed up in the tree several times, he said things like, "You know, this is our secret hideout. We're hiding up here and we can't tell anybody about it. Especially your parents." This process of being secretive and constantly manipulating me with repetitive information was his way of getting me to think like him. During World War II, not every German lined up with Hitler. Indeed, a majority probably didn't agree with what going on in concentration camps. However, because of brainwashing, they either remained oblivious to what was going on or were too afraid to object.

In the same way, this cunning teen cultivated our friendship to gather more knowledge of my likes and dislikes. Once he had convinced me that we should keep our playhouse a secret, he might add reinforcement, like asking, "What are you afraid of?" or reminding me, "You know, you can't tell your parents what we do up here. That just wouldn't be right." I remember playing this one game that included colors like green, yellow, blue, red, black, and white. We would roll the dice and if I landed on a certain color I would lose, which meant I would have to perform a sexual act on him or have one performed on me. I wasn't very good at this game because I constantly lost (I can still see those colors.)

Dazed and Confused

This kind of experience was horribly confusing, especially at a young age. I wasn't being beaten, nor was this guy mean to me. Still, it just didn't feel right. If there was nothing wrong, why did he want me to keep everything a secret? Looking back, it makes me sick to my stomach. But at the time, I had all these layers of fear and manipulation that I would have had to fight through. As a young boy, I didn't have the courage, nor did I know how to express to anyone else what was happening. We only lived in that area for nine months, which is one instance where Mom's constant relocations removed me from a bad situation. I hate to think what might have happened if we had lived there for years.

Nor was I alone. While the memory is vague, around the same time of my first molestation experiences, I remember playing doctor with Barbie dolls belonging to a girl my age and GI Joe figures that belonged to me or her younger brother. And we would have the dolls of both genders engage in sexual acts. The only way a child that young gets involved in such stuff is if someone else has already acted out their perverse desires on him or her.

Not surprisingly, by the time I reached first grade, an unhealthy appetite had festered inside me. Susie, a girl one year older than me, had been exposed to similar influences. Whoever thinks that living in a small town is going to automatically shield children from perversion or other societal problems should wake up and smell the coffee. The town where we lived then had two taverns, a grocery store the size of a postage stamp, a Laundromat, and a carwash. And there in my first-grade year, I went out behind one of those taverns with Susie. There in the brush and trees we would play house. Once we tried to have sex, but it didn't work.

Susie and I kept in touch for years because my older sister was married to her brother. We bumped into each other at various family gatherings, but after my sister's divorce, my friendship with Susie faded away. I wish I had had a chance to find out more about what had adversely affected her at such a young age. But this wasn't the kind of subject that either of us cared to bring up over Thanksgiving turkey. The topic is so sensitive and so personal that most people never wanted to acknowledge they were the victim of abuse. Recently a counseling opportunity brought me in touch with a fifty-six-year-old man who had been molested and raped as a child. He had never told anyone about it, and when he confided in me, the tears came gushing out with the force of a waterfall. The fact that I had been victimized more than once as a child established a common bond between us.

On another occasion, I counseled a young woman who refused to open up until I said, "I understand why you cut yourself because I have the scars from where I used to do that because it helped relieve the pain of my messed-up life." When I showed her the scars on my arms, she started bawling. My self-cutting originated with a pervert who had groomed me more than forty years earlier. It may sound impossible that anything good can emerge from such tragedy, but the fact that I am able to help console and encourage molestation victims today is just one example of the possibilities of overcoming the past.

Victimized Again

Unfortunately, my experience with molestation didn't end when we moved away from that home with the tree house. Several years later, my stepfather's cousin played the same cruel games as the teenager who victimized me in kindergarten. This guy lived next to an apple orchard. When he got tired of whatever game we were playing, he would take me over to the orchard (I can still smell the fruit and the fresh spring breezes.) There were ladders set up against the trees. He invented another game where if I didn't hustle up the ladder in time, I would lose. I lost a lot.

One day, my parents and I went over to my stepfather's parents' house so they could sit and talk while they smoked cigarettes. My stepfather's cousin often hung around there. When all the adults decided to take off for the grocery store, they left the two us alone. Before I knew what had happened, we were back out in the orchard. This guy was a master manipulator, always playing on my emotions and persuading me to feel sorry for him because he was deaf. He would play with my feelings as if I were a puppet on a marionette's strings, leading me step by step. The next thing I knew, I was doing something I didn't want to, but in my confusion and the chaos of my background, I had no solid grasp of the difference between right and wrong. Nor did I know how to get out of the situation, leaving me a sitting duck for trouble. However, by the time I reached sixth grade, I had enough presence of mind and awareness of sexual matters to know this just wasn't right. When he started in again, I screamed, "Dude! Get away from me!" and ran away. He didn't follow, and I never saw him again.

Such experiences inflicted long-lasting damage and left me with a distorted impression of intimacy. In my mind, love and sex were two different, unconnected things. Not until years later did I understand that sex flows out of the intimacy you develop with another person. It is natural to have sexual relations with your spouse because of the love you have for each other. You can't separate love and intimacy. Society wants to pretend that sex is no big deal, inventing phrases like "friends with benefits" (and it's often the guy who enjoys the benefits while the girl is oblivious to how she's being used).

The worst thing is how kids quickly pick up on what is happening while adults pretend the kids don't recognize the truth—or that it won't bother them. Recently I heard about a couple who decided they would have an "open" relationship where they would be free to form sexual liaisons with other people and remain married to each other. After observing the strange comings and goings of her parents, and mysterious people appearing from time to time at their house, their daughter told a friend, "When I grow up, I want to be a whore like my mother."

The Danger of Permissiveness

Because of my past, I am probably more sensitive to the damage sexual permissiveness is doing to the most vulnerable members of society. One of the most obvious examples is our lax attitudes about pornography, which wrecks countless marriages and leaves people feeling isolated, disconnected, and prone to failure. Once the province of seedy adult movie theaters, it is now readily available online and on demand in millions of homes. Nor does it occur in a vacuum: pornography is just one aspect of a sex industry that the National Institutes of Health (NIH) estimates (as of 2012) is a $57 billion business worldwide, generating $15 billion annually in the US alone. Pornographers have more than profits from X-rated movies. They also want to lure viewers to visit strip clubs and purchase lap dances or sexual favors. According to the NIH says the US has

- more strip clubs than any other country in the world;
- more than 3,800 adult clubs nationwide that employ over 500,000 people;
- more women employed in the sex industry than in any other point in time.

In addition, between 66 and 90 percent of women in the sex industry were sexually abused as children. Plus, relative to the general population, these women experience higher rates of substance abuse, sexually transmitted diseases, domestic violence, depression, violent assault, rape, and posttraumatic stress disorder.[1]

One NIH report notes that only recently have researchers looked into violence against women working in this industry because of a long-held assumption most do so willingly and are somehow shielded from sexual and physical harm. Studies have shown that both "indoor" (such as strip joints or cabarets) and "outdoor" (prostitution or escort services) sex work increases a woman's risk of being assaulted. Two researchers found that found that 82 percent of women engaged in prostitution report being physically assaulted; 68 percent say they have been raped. More than half of the exotic dancers report they have been threatened with a weapon.

Far from being voluntary, many women involved in this seamy side of life and who have experienced trauma feel shattered and hopeless. The report's authors wrote: "Some escape the lifestyle, yet with limited resources many find themselves 'trapped' in the business. Many have been attacked, exploited, and humiliated, and mind-altering substances often are sought to temporarily mollify the physical and emotional pain. The most prevalent mental health symptoms are in the mood and anxiety spectrums, but are often coupled with addiction to substances. Many of these women who use substances state they are anesthetizing themselves to be able to work in the sex industry. Posttraumatic stress disorder (PTSD) is widespread in this subset of the population and usually is attributed to childhood abuse and/or sex industry-related trauma. A substantial number of these women are homeless single mothers of multiple children, under-educated, and medically uninsured; have a high rate of untreated health-related problems; and often have legal problems."[2]

Such victims include Harmony Dust, the author of *Scars and Stilettos*, an account of overcoming childhood trauma that eventually led to a career as a stripper. In an account of her life, she wrote about one of her earliest memories from childhood: her father watching porn in the bed next to her during a weekend visit when she was only three or four. Although he moved out of the state a couple years later and she rarely saw him after that, other people picked up where he left off. She tells of being sexually abused by multiple men and women throughout her life.

"The abuse left me filled with shame and anger towards myself," she says. "I thought that something was inherently wrong with me that kept attracting that kind of attention. When I was 13, my mom's boyfriend moved in with us. She met him in a Narcotics Anonymous meeting after he fled Canada in order to escape statutory rape charges for having sex with a minor. He made sexual advance towards me in front of my mother and even went so far as to tell her he was in love with me. I told my mom that her boyfriend kept coming in my room at night and asked her to stop him. She explained that if I wore long pants and stopped practicing my dance routines in the living room, this wouldn't be happening. Through all of this I learned from her that it was my responsibility to try to control other people's sexual responses towards me."[3]

Not surprisingly, in her late teens, Harmony wound up in a cruel and abusive relationship, deeply in debt, and so cowed by her boyfriend that she didn't object when he started openly sleeping around. So when someone promised she could make a small fortune as an exotic dancer, she quickly seized the opportunity. For three years, she lived a "double life," dancing in a fully-nude strip joint, performing under the name of Monique. However, she later escaped that lifestyle and now works as an activist to help free other women from the clutches of the sex industry.

Legion of Abuse

Were Harmony's story an isolated incident, you could pass it off as some kind of strange aberration. But there are legions of stories of women abused as children. Just one more example is the sad story of Carol Rogers. Sexually abused by her stepfather at the age of five, she started stealing at the age of nine, skipping school at eleven, and a year later, advanced to drinking alcohol and then using marijuana. Because she was out of control, her mother took her to work with her—at a nightclub. Surrounded by exotic dancers and prostitutes, Carol learned how to make money. "I was taught how to drink and feel good, and loosen up; we took pills at first," she says. "I drank a lot. By the age of fifteen I was doing it on my own and selling my body… I was always hurting myself. I cut my wrists. That's how I released the pain."[4]

If you read in chapter 1 how I used to cut myself as a child for the same reason, you can appreciate how deeply her story resonates with me. There are far too many examples of broken and dysfunctional homes that can be traced back to sexual immorality to pretend that it doesn't exist. It is the elephant in the living room that American society largely refuses to acknowledge. Maybe because it illustrates the moral erosion damaging our nation; the truth behind that is no unpleasant that many people don't want to confront it.

This can be seen in ways large and small. During my Army career, young guys in the barracks would talk about the porn industry as a career choice. To them, acting in X-rated films was "no big deal." Society had hammered that message into their heads for so long they couldn't see that anything was wrong with it. In our schools, sex education is working its way down into earlier and earlier grades, under the guise of teaching children to accept their sexuality as a normal part of life. The trouble is, without a corresponding message about the proper framework in which sexual relations should occur, all such classes accomplish is teaching kids more ways to have sex. Premarital sex is a fact of life in middle schools now. In the same way those young Army privates looked at porn as no big deal, children at progressively younger ages have a casual view of sex.

I don't want to sound like an alarmist. If we take a realistic look at sexual practices in our nation in the past, one reason fewer people had premarital sex is so many got married at a younger age. Nor were our ancestors pure as the driven snow. Two centuries ago, 10 percent of American brides were pregnant before marriage, a rate that didn't rise that high again until late in the twentieth century.[5] In more recent times, my mother first married at sixteen and her brother tied the knot before his eighteenth birthday.

What concerns me is the spreading of permissive attitudes, which especially affect young people. One time I caught my then-teenage son looking at porn on his computer. I did my best not to treat him like some kind of freak or make him feel so bad the only thing I would accomplish is convincing him he should hide this activity from me. "You're setting yourself for danger," I told him. "When you watch this kind of stuff, you will find it starting with one guy and one girl. The next time, it might be two girls and one guy, or two girls, and by the time you're an age where you ready for a marital relationship, you will have distorted views of what intimacy is all about."

Having lived through the problems that come with unhealthy sexual activity at too early an age, I always encourage parents to maintain open dialogues with their children, no matter how young they may be. Warn them that if anyone does certain things that make them uncomfortable or frighten them, that they should never be afraid to come and tell you about it. Also, let them know if someone does something to them, the person at fault is the one who did it—not the child. Be very skeptical about someone older who wants to associate with them. If your child is five or six years old and a teenager wants to go outside and play with your child on a regular basis, be very wary. If you have a sixth-grader and a twenty-two-year-old wants to go outside and play cars with him, something is wrong. No normal twenty-two-year old will want to do that.

Children are innocent, tender-hearted, and susceptible to those who want to prey on them. For the sake of their future, I hope you will guard against what happened to me from happening to them.

Notes

1. Innovations in Clinical Neuroscience, Table 1, http://www.ncbi.nlm.nih.gov/pmc/articles/PMC3508959/table/T1/.
2. Ariz Anklesaria and Julie P. Gentile, MD, "Psychotherapy with Women Who Have Worked in the 'Sex Industry,'" Innovations in Clinical Science, October 2012, http://www.ncbi.nlm.nih.gov/pmc/articles/PMC3508959/.
3. "Our Founder," Treasures, http://iamatreasure.com/our-stories/harmonys-story/#sthash.aygkK0Dx.dpbs.
4. "Wild Girl Gone Good," Christian Broadcasting Network, http://www.cbn.com/tv/1410273553001.
5. "Family Life: Courtship and Marriage," http://www.encyclopedia.com/doc/1G2-2536601450.html.

CHAPTER 5
The Foundation of Discipline

Discipline may seem like a dirty word in a casual, do-whatever-makes-you-feel good world. But only with discipline can you overcome a lackadaisical attitude to life that won't take you far. Nor does discipline necessarily mean an existence characterized by drudgery and endlessly repeating the same old routine. It can mean the excitement of taking advantage of information that is clearly available to everyone. Yet only with discipline will you see the see the opportunity and capitalize on it.

My firsthand lesson in this reality came after I had left full-time military service, planning to stay in the National Guard to finish my Army career. A good buddy and I got recruited from First Corp at Fort Lewis (which later merged with the McChord Air Force Base and today is known as Joint Base Lewis-McChord). The Santa Fe, New Mexico–based Burlington-Northern Railroad needed reliable employees to replace an aging and retiring crew. This meant passing a federal hazmat (hazardous materials) test, which is such a massive examination they struggled to find people who could pass it. To be a conductor, you had to score 90 percent or above on the hazardous material test, pass a drug test, and exhibit the kind of character that convinced them you would show up for work on time (another example of the value of discipline).

I completed five months of training with the railroad, the first portion was in Kansas City (if my memory serves me well, this was back in 1998) the next four months was in the Northwest (Seattle-Tacoma Area) where we received hands on training. Every job has its drawbacks; this one was dropping everything at a moment's notice when they wanted you to go somewhere. Still, I passed the test and got my license to become a bonafide conductor for the railroad. However, after the grueling preparations involved, the day after I obtained my license, the railroad furloughed me, which means they laid me off from work. This is how I wound up in the ironic position of returning to Fort Lewis. I had spent more than six years there during fulltime military service, and now I found myself as a contract worker.

Though I had no idea how the long this job would last, it was fulltime and essentially involved doing whatever your supervisor asked you to do. The

Army Major I worked for called one day and ask me to do a report he forgot to complete (he had to attend a conference); I agreed. I completed the report and turned it in the Colonel. When it came back, it had two red marks on it that I had to fix; I addressed the discrepancies and turned it back in. Then I didn't hear anything else—until several Captains and Majors showed up at my small office, asking, "What did you do? I was concerned at first, I thought I did something wrong. Then they asked me, 'How did you get your report back with only two errors? Every time we get our stuff, there's red marks all over the place.' What did you do?"

"What do you mean, what did I do?" I said several times. I was told to write a report, and I wrote a report. What do you guys do?"

Then they began to explain the convoluted process they followed that included using a lot of gobbledygook and military language they thought would sound good. But when they turned in their report to the Colonel, he usually sent it back full of red marks. They would redo it, sometimes three, four, or five times. *So how did I get by with two marks and one revision?*

At first, I thought they were kidding. After all, I had every Army manual on the eight CDs they had handed me on my first day on the job. The major had asked me to write a report related to the Army National Guard and Army Reserves as it related to their active duty counterpart. The question I needed to answer in the report and was sent to the Colonel for review prior to the General's meeting was: How can the Army National Guard and the Army Reserves support First Corps with their latest mission? All that meant was researching the different manuals, cutting and pasting information, changing dates and times, and rewriting sentences so they flowed together and read coherently. Then turn it in.

"Why are you guys making stuff up?" I asked. "The Army has already written it for you."

This experience shows how discipline is ready to respond when duty calls and take advantage of resources already at hand to complete a task.

Discipline Meets Duty

There's more. Another time, the Major came up to me and said, "Hey, the General wants to conduct First Corps FTX." FTX is Army-speak for field training exercise. What the Major was tasked with was finding a facility that would accommodate sixty to seventy soldiers during the General's operations order briefing (an operations order is like writing a business plan for combat purposes). "He needs to have a facility that will accommodate both good weather and inclement weather," the Major continued. "Then, if it's nice weather, we can have it outdoors."

I was sure the computer rifle qualification range would work, I replied, "Go out to Range 36, by the C-5 mock-up, they already have a facility that will work."

"Will it hold seventy people?" he asked.

"I believe so," I replied. Still, he asked me to double-check so he would feel comfortable informing the Colonel of this location. This was a reasonable request; I was not positive if the indoor seating area would accommodate seventy soldiers. I drove out to the range, confirmed the seating situation, and reported my observations to the Major. The outdoor seating would hold about 120 soldiers, while the capacity of the indoor seating held about half that—meaning lower-ranking officers and non-commissioned officer (NCO) would have to stand. The room itself could hold between seventy-five and eighty-five soldiers. While the Major felt this would be a good location, he wanted to know if I thought any other locations would work.

"I was stationed here not long ago, for more than six years, as an 18-B (Special Forces Weapons Sergeant), and I have used every range Fort Lewis has," I said. "This is the best location for what the General is requesting."

However, after the Major informed the Colonel, it didn't satisfy the Colonel. The Colonel wanted me to drive to other ranges to ensure that this was the best and most suitable location. I drove to five specific ranges to check those locations. On the way, I drove past 60 percent of the other ranges, then reported to the Major that range 36, by the C-5 mock-up, provides the facilities that meet the General's request: "There are no other ranges that will provide an inclement and outdoor seating area that will hold seventy soldiers." Convinced, the Major informed the Colonel—who still wasn't satisfied and asked me to look again. Although there were ranges at North Fort Lewis, I knew they would not accommodate the General's request. After three more exchanges, I felt myself getting quite frustrated with the Colonel and told the Major, "The Colonel can look himself because I obviously am not qualified to locate this range."

"Neither I, nor you, have the rank to inform the Colonel of your request," he replied. "Just try one more time."

My frustration was epic by this point; I decided to write a special reconnaissance report. This was the kind of report Special Forces teams would compile when we had to execute a special reconnaissance mission. This comprehensive report included aerial photographs, ground photos, sketches, maps, and a written report on the target of interest. It evaluated strengths and weaknesses of the location—the strengths and weaknesses included vulnerabilities, enemy capabilities, equipment, and other items. So that's what I did, writing a report that included sketches of the facility, aerial photographs I obtained from First Group, and some pictures I took and had printed at a one-hour photo shop. I even purchased plastic covers to hold copies of the final product. I doubt anyone had ever written such a complete report on this facility, but I wanted it to look as professional as possible.

It went all the way up to the General. His reaction: "This is now the new standard."

Truthfully, I not only felt honored but a bit amused. Had my findings not been repeatedly challenged, I wouldn't have compiled such an extensive study. Still, thanks to the discipline I had learned in Special Forces, I was ready to respond to an unrealistic demand with the kind of effort and details that captured a General's attention. Now, the General never came to my office—or the Colonel—to give either of us a pat on the back. But I still had the satisfaction of knowing that, thanks to my Special Forces training and discipline, I had done the finest possible job in a frustrating situation.

I say all this because the training and disciple one has will go a long way in one's success. Today, our society everybody gets a trophy and there is no winner or loser. This is not teaching discipline to our children; this is not teaching work ethics to our children—this is not teaching our children the satisfaction of earning something! One of the issues that are society has today is in the definition of discipline, the practice of training people to obey rules or a code of behavior, using punishment to correct this obedience. Let's break this down a little bit. First let's look at obeying rules; today, people make up their own rules. It's a feel-good society. A young person I finished talking to the other day was complaining about a DUI (driving under the influence) that he received. First, he stated that the police officer had no legitimate reason to pull him over, that he had to make something up. "The policeman said I drove over the yellow line in the center of the road, and I did not," he adamantly expressed. "Then the police officer asked me why I had empty beer cans in the back of my car and asked me to step out of the vehicle. I again told him that they are empty beer cans and I've not been drinking."

Then this young man expressed, with disdain in his voice, "The officer told me, 'Then you have nothing to worry about, young man.'" To make a long story short, this young man blew a .08, which is the minimum requirement for the DUI in Washington state. I wish this young man had the discipline to accept responsibility for what he's done; two years later, maybe even three, he still does not accept responsibility and blames it on the officer. I no longer get into this conversation with this young man because I only get frustrated. But I did overhear him talking to my wife and expressed his dissatisfaction in the man (the police) as he stated. He told my wife, "I should have never gotten pulled over, and why do they have a rule that .08 is acceptable and if I blew a .08, why did I go to jail?"

While my wife has a little bit more patience than I do and in this case, much more wisdom. She told this young man, "If you would have never been drinking and then choosing to get behind the wheel and drive, you would've never been put into the situation with the police officer. In the city that we live in," she continues, "we have free taxi service for people were drinking. Why did you not use them?"

He stopped talking to my wife and never answered the question. Discipline is not just obeying the rules; it's also accepting responsibility when we break these rules. In this particular case, this young man did not obey the rules or the code of behavior is acceptable by our society and did not want to accept the punishment that was imposed upon him. The punishment that was imposed upon him, he is forced to accept or more punishment will come this way. But this is a society of everybody's a winner; we don't teach our children discipline, hard work.

The foundation of discipline is first learning if it's worthwhile, if it takes work, and if it's free, it's not good. The foundation of discipline that I learned was a long time ago, young and my age. You guys learned throughout this book that my mom moved a lot; consequently, I moved as well. Academically, I struggled, but athletically, I was better than most. Anytime we moved to a new area, I knew I wasn't going to win people over my intellectual abilities, but rather my athletic abilities. You might ask how this plays out, but you play pick-up football games, play tag, whatever it might be. I remember when we moved to Grandview the first time, I was in fifth grade, and there was a park with an irrigation ditch next to it. All the older kids try to jump the ditch and clear the water. Most of them were about three or four grade levels above me; I was in fifth grade. I watch these kids trying to jump this irrigation ditch; most of them didn't make it, some did. I needed to make new friends; I walked over the parking lot, and as this one boy was getting ready to run and jump it, much older than me, I went flying past him running as fast as I could, jumping the ditch, clearing it and then some. Again, you may be asking, what does this have to do with discipline? At that moment in my fifth-grade year, I realized I was faster than most. I could jump higher than most and jump further than most. So as I grew up, I concentrated and was discipline in athletics. I played football, ran track in high school, and year round, I trained in martial arts. I was a pretty good football player, I had about seven scholarships or letters from colleges and universities that were interested in me playing for them; however, I was a little small for a football player in the eighties—five-foot-nine and 160 pounds. I was good enough in the long jump and triple jump that I was invited to participate with the International Sports Exchange, where our track team competed in China.

The discipline that I gained in football, track, and martial arts carried over into my adult life. One thing I can say, if you're reading this book and run this chapter in this particular moment is, if your child does not like education, does not want to participate in school, find something that they can do, such as sports, and push them to develop the discipline it takes to be the best they can be. They may not always be the best at what they're doing, but if they have the discipline to be the best they can be, this will develop the discipline they need in the future to be the best at whatever they do in their chosen career. What I am saying, because I was good at sports, being a good athlete, I knew I had to have a 2.0 or C average in order to participate in high school sports. Because of this requirement by the school and because I wanted to play sports, I maintained a 2.0 GPA (I think I graduated like a 2.5 or something) and graduated from high school. My wife is currently an English teacher at one of our local high schools, and because of the sports or extracurricular activities that these children want to participate in, they maintained this requirement established by the school in order to play the sports that they wish.

An example of what I mean by this is when one of the students in my wife's class was receiving a failing grade, he talked to her about his grade and asked how he could bring it up so we could play a particular sport. She told him, "You need to make up your back assignments, do your work, and turn your work in on time." She said that she would work with him on his makeup assignments, but she would not give him special treatment or special privileges. The young man made up his assignments and is now receiving an acceptable GPA in order to play sports. Now this is the following year (the issue with his grades happened the year prior, his freshman year) and he developed the discipline in his studies to maintain the GPA requirements in his school to play sports. You may think that this discipline he has developed is only because he wants to play sports, but it will carry through the rest of his life if he maintains this positive foundation of discipline. His foundational effort for discipline, which he developed today, will be a foundation that impacts his future.

Finally, we are looking at discipline. Discipline is the act of training oneself to achieve things that will benefit them in the long run. You've all read chapter 2 of the roots, and the roots that are established by abuse are life-lasting. In turn, the roots that we establish the discipline and the actions of achieving something by working for creating this discipline that will help us in the long run is establishing a positive root system for the rest of your life. A lot of people look at discipline as being painful hard work. "Oh my gosh, this is going to suck," one might say, but in the long run, it'll pay off. When we could even see in Scripture that God teaches us this: he knows it's not easy, but it does pay off. Let's look at Hebrews, chapter 12 verse 11 (ESV), "For the moment all discipline seems painful rather than pleasant, but later it yields the peaceful fruit of righteousness to those who have been trained by it." Not only does this talk about having good fruit of what we've done through the discipline, but this also tells us that we're training in this process. Anything worthwhile, anything worth keeping, anything of value takes time, takes hard work, and takes discipline to achieve the goal one set.

"Successful people do what unsuccessful people don't do" (Ester Spina).

One of the issues I have when it comes to discipline is that everyone understands the meaning of discipline, but very few execute it. Successful people understand discipline, and they incorporate discipline into their daily lives. It is so true what Ester Spina said, "Successful people do what unsuccessful people don't do." There are plenty of people with talent, but very few people have the discipline to do what it takes to stand out in the crowed. You look at any person that has made great accomplishments in their lives, such as professional athletes, CEOs, college professors, special operations operator, they all had the talent to achieve their goals (their success) and all had the discipline to do what it took to get there.

One of the issues people have when it comes to discipline is effort; it takes effort to be disciplined, but I guess that is the point—nothing comes from nothing. The other issue is people's accountability; if a person is disciplined, they follow rules. They are held accountable for their actions. Some may disagree, a business owner is not accountable for his or her actions; they are the boss. Well, that is not true; despite the fact they are held accountable to the government and the laws of the land, they are held accountable to their customers. The business must have the dedication and discipline to do his or her job every day even if they do not have a boss. When a person is disciplined to his or her responsibilities, they build structure, stability, pride (not being prideful, but proud of what they have accomplished), positive life habits in their life, just to name a few. Just think about it, if everyone was in it for themselves and had no discipline, people would become lawless, doing whatever felt good to them and no consideration for others.

Have you ever been in a store and in the line there is a person with very little self-discipline? They do and say whatever they feel; they have very little self-restraint. I know for myself; I have had this happen more than a few times. I just cringe, hoping I do not line up in their crosshairs. One day about a year ago, I was in line, and this person was so angry she had very little restraint and bad-mouthed the cashier. I was in shock. I got in the line at the same time she did and the cashier did nothing to warrant this attack. Well, I put my stuff on the conveyer belt, and when her last item was picked up by the cashier, my stuff moved down. She then looked at me and started expressing her dissatisfaction with my intrusion on her space. I told her she was not a nice lady, and she should apologize to the cashier for her own exclamatory she expressed to the cashier. She became angrier with me and started cursing at me. I finally told her to shut up, and she said, "You would not talk to your grandmother like that" (she was an older lady). I told her, "My grandmother was dead!" She did not know how to respond to me and turned her back to me and left shortly after. The cashier thanked me for sticking up for her and was hurt by the lady. God tells us to be kind to one another, be tender-hearted, forgive each other, just as He has forgiven us (Ephesians 4:32). We may not always handle situations well, but if we have a disciplined life, we will often handle situations correctly and in a way that will represent God.

As you have read and will continue to read in this book, you are gaining knowledge. Have the disciple to use the knowledge you gain; this will demonstrate your wisdom. To many times people have mass amounts of knowledge, but they don't use it. It takes disciple to change things. We all make New Year resolutions, but very few of us have the disciple to follow through with the resolution we made, me being one of them.

Young Boy

Seaside, WA Vacation

1986 Graduation

Promotion to Sergeant

Posing in Saudi Arabia

Iraq 1990-1991 Gulf War

82nd Scout Platoon

Me and Mom

Special Forces

Winter Warfare Training

Tonga 1996

Menton Day, 1st Special Forces Group

Rehearsal Before Helocast

Last Military Photo

My First Month as a Pastor

Baptising Someone in India

Church in India

Teresa and I in Hawaii

CHAPTER 6

The Foundation of Faith

Until the night my middle son, Hunter, flat-lined as he turned blue, I never considered there might be more to this universe and its operations. A power greater than me at work in our lives. After all, I was a lean, mean, fighting machine. I was intelligent, tough, and in control—or so I thought.

The crisis erupted in the middle of the last part of my specialized army training. The Special Forces Qualification Course is informally known as the Q course. This mind-bending exercise wraps up with an isolation test that requires trainees to memorize a book thicker than the average phone directory. After all, when you fight the bad guys, you can't carry a three-ring binder into battle to see which way you're supposed to go, how much ground you should cover, or where to set up a base of operations. Mastering this course included outlining a set of four plans: (1) primary, (2) alternate, (3) contingency, and (4) emergency. If you are parachuting in, you have to detail the same kind of approach for four drop zones.

Just as I was in the midst of cramming for the iso (short for isolation) exam, I got a call: "Your newborn son has some serious health issues." Hunter had already sent the monitors beeping several times. My heart leaped into my throat. After my instructor agreed to give me a ride, I dropped my gear and jumped into his jeep. Then we hightailed it to the hospital at Fort Bragg, North Carolina. When I arrived, nurses rushed me into the intensive care unit. They didn't think Hunter was going to make it. Despite the pale blue tinge of his skin, he survived the first night. I stayed at his side, grabbing coffee occasionally, although nervous tension gave me more of an adrenaline rush than the caffeine.

The next morning, my commander gave me an option. I could recycle and pick up where I left off with the next class, or continue on and someone would bring me back to the hospital each evening so I could stay with my former wife and be with my son, Hunter. The enormity of the decision fell over my shoulders like the weight of a two-ton barbell. I was competing for the number one spot in our class against two other guys; all three of us were within a hundredth of a percentage point of each other. And I didn't want to lose my chance to finish on top. After all, it had been a grueling ordeal to get this far.

In the military, you have to qualify at several levels on your way to the commandant's list. When you make these lists, it winds up on your official records and means you may get promoted faster. That is, if you obtain satisfactory evaluations and meet other criteria. While this may sound routine to a non-military person, leaving a class and picking it up later is infinitely harder than dropping out of a bonehead English course your freshman year of college. So even though I could recycle into another class, I wanted to maintain my standing in the current session and compete for honor graduate. With a ninety-six-plus grade average, I stood a pretty good chance.

However, the primary motivation for staying in the class stemmed from the assignment that would follow with the First Special Forces Group at Fort Lewis, Washington. Hunter's mother and I was from Washington. Not only did we think it would be a good place to raise our family, Special Forces duties would require regular travel. Since I would be gone a lot, it would be much better for her and our children to be close to extended family. If I recycled into the next class, I did not know if I would still get assigned to Fort Lewis.

Balancing all these considerations was the fact that right now, *my family needed me*. No one had ever given me a manual for dealing with this kind of life-and-death dilemma. Shaken to the core, I wondered if there was anything to some of those Bible stories I heard occasionally in my childhood. However, once I gathered my wits, I shook it off and kept moving. I stayed in the course and returned to the hospital every night. My former spouse at the time and I agreed to this approach so we could maintain our path toward Washington. That desire helped me stay focused, especially when the time came for the isolation test. I'm not sure of the exact number, but as I remember, there were hundreds of questions. No multiple choice: A, B, C, D, or E, but fill-in-the-blank questions like, "What are the grid coordinates for your infiltration location?" If you didn't know it, you couldn't fake it.

Life Changes

Hunter survived the ordeal, but our marriage didn't. We rushed into marriage when I was twenty-one and my first wife was nineteen, after planning our wedding in about ten days. The Army recruiter told me, "If you're planning on marrying this girl and you get married before you leave, then you'll get more money on your housing allowance." So on Valentine's Day, we tied the knot at the nearest Salvation Army. When problems arose, we didn't know how to work them out. The sad part of divorce is, you don't separate from your spouse; the noncustodial parent also separates from the children.

Still, I can see how God used the desperation and anguish I felt after my divorce, which prompted me to transfer to the Washington National Guard. They assigned me to the Nineteenth Special Forces Group, the first of several changes before I completed my military career as a recruiter. Despite the chaos and drinking that characterized my life, when a friend first suggested I visit his church, I thought, "Yeah, right. You can forget it, buddy." The only time I had attended church was in first grade and only Sunday school. Later, I went to mass occasionally at a Catholic church, but only because my girlfriend was a Catholic. I wasn't interested in what the priest had to say, and I sure didn't want anyone sprinkling holy water (or any other kind) on me. Ironically, as I look back on that early exposure to God, I can see how He used to it to lay a spiritual foundation in my life.

I also remember the time I worked part-time at a restaurant in my hometown. My mother owned a cafe, but nobody wants to work for their mother. Still, her connections in the business helped me land a part-time gig at another restaurant. The cook there was a Christian and would talk to me about his faith. Wanting to carry on a conversation, I would discuss the Bible, although I had no idea what in the world I was talking about. Finally, during one of our chats, he asked what church I attended. When I told him I didn't, he asked if I read the Bible.

"No," I said, "I generally don't read books."

"Well, how do you know much?"

"Well, I don't."

Then, as my eyes grew wide with surprise, he delivered what he later called a "prophecy," declaring that someday I would be a preacher.

Then I forgot about that encounter, until years later. After leaving the military, I wound up becoming a business banker. It was a miracle that I ever got hired, since I only had a two-year associate's degree and no banking experience. Yet US Bank still hired me for the position. Among my many customers was Tom, the associate pastor of a church. Tom would drop in every week to deposit the Sunday offerings. More than once at the end of a conversation, he would ask, "When are you coming to church?" Knowing he wouldn't take offense, I would reply, "I ain't going to church." As our friendship grew, whenever he asked, I would say things like, "C'mon. You're all a bunch of hypocrites." These exchanges turned into a kind of game. He would harass me, and I would harass him back, but he never quit asking.

He also kept making small points about God, working tidbits of biblical wisdom into our conversations, or telling me about the joy of knowing Christ. I later heard a pastor compare churches to hamburgers. "They're all the same," he said. "McDonald's, Burger King, Jack in the Box, Carl's Junior, Zips—they're all the same, just different flavors. That's like churches, just different flavors. But the person that goes in there isn't a Zips' employee, or a McDonald's employee, he's a Christian. So with non-Christians, you just keep feeding them hamburgers. They may decide they like someone else's hamburgers and go to somebody else's church, who will also feed them hamburgers. Eventually, they'll get so full on hamburgers they become part of it."

Likewise, if you have a foundation of faith and continuing contact with somebody outside the church, just keep feeding them the hamburgers and eventually they will "get it." They're going to decide they need the spiritual nourishment that only God can offer. That's what happened to me. Tom kept feeding me until I reached the point of fullness—that moment of decision where I thought, "Maybe there is something to this stuff after all." I kept thinking back to the tough-guy methods I used to stuff down the emotions of dealing with Hunter's near-death experience, and how they only could deliver a momentary relief before my doubts resurfaced. One day, Tom walked in to my office and said, "When are you coming to church?" I blinked my eyes and hesitated momentarily before I replied, "Fine, I'll go. But you can't ask again."

Life Changes

I found myself attracted to this church because the pastor's aggressive nature reflected mine. I went for a couple months, often showing up late because I didn't care for the music (it wasn't the grunge and heavy metal I liked). Still, the more I heard, the more rational the pastor sounded. I didn't know the Holy Spirit was drawing me like a flame beckons to a moth. Drawn to the church initially because I could relate to the pastor, the more I attended, the more the Holy Spirit worked on me. As the weeks passed, I started showing up earlier—turns out I liked the worship music after all. After about two months of going, Teresa (my wife) and I decided the time had come and committed ourselves to the Lord, Jesus Christ.

One morning during service, the pastor asked, "If anybody wants to receive Jesus as your Lord and Savior, come down front," I thought, *Yeah, I want to do this. It's time to turn over the reins of my life to God.* Teresa went with me, and soon after, four of my five children made the same decision. A month later, we were all baptized together. My other son eventually made the decision to be baptized. Whether you say I found the Lord or the Lord found me is irrelevant. I believe God calls out to every individual; the only choice is whether you will answer. Since almost everyone has a smart phone (or at least a cell phone with caller ID) now, they can see who is calling and decide whether to answer it.

My experience shows the inherent value of friendship and how a follower of Christ helps others make the choice to join God's family. Had it not been for Tom and him reaching out to me prior to my conversion, I don't know if I would have gone to church a second time. Tom was a good friend and would always call me on a Friday or Saturday to chat, see how I was doing, and ask whether I needed anything. In the process he would slip in—in a casual sort of way—whether I was going to church on Sunday. His action taught me that if I want to lead someone to Christ, I need to become their friend and show them the love of Jesus through my actions, not empty lip service.

Tom helped me answer the call. Now, God had been calling to me since first grade, but for years, Jose Cuervo looked like a better god to me. Before I made the decision to follow Jesus, every Friday night, I would buy two-fifths of rum and another of tequila. After putting away a bunch of it, I would go out partying. Then I would drink up the rest of the liquor on Saturday. Sometimes, I would have to buy more liquor on Saturday because I drank it all up on Friday night.

If you can imagine, after getting hammered on Friday night, I sometimes ran eight miles on Saturday. Not only did that help me sober up, it got a lot of the alcohol out of my system. This isn't an exaggeration. I used to see guys in the military put away a fifth or two of whiskey and go on a ten-mile hike the next day. I still remember a report from my time at Fort Bragg that called one of the airborne infantry units there "the most fit alcoholics in the world."

New Patterns

This describes the pattern of many of my old army buddies. I loved having fun with these guys and how they always seemed to love having a good time. But this God over here I heard about occasionally sounded like a cosmic killjoy. He didn't seem to want people to have any fun. Ever. All the church folks I knew (truthfully, only a small handful) seemed more hung up on keeping a long list of rules than loving others. Occasionally I heard some guy yakking on the radio who didn't sound very loving either. So I judged God based on what others said.

In the past, I assumed if I made a decision to follow Christ, I would first have to wade through a bunch of criticism, judgment, or "I told you so's." I thought if I went to some church, I would have to give up everything I knew. I found that was not the case at all. My new life would not be measured by what I gave up, but what I gained. When I answered the phone, I discovered God had a new life waiting for me, one more rewarding and filled with joy than I ever thought possible. The day I responded to God's call, I confessed my belief in Jesus as His Son and that His death on the cross had made it possible for me to enjoy eternal life in heaven. I agreed that I wanted to turn my back on my old life because the drunkenness, anger, and self-centeredness that went with it weren't worth hanging onto anyway.

I compare it to dating. When I talked to God and He talked back to me, it felt like the thrill of meeting that special person. Anyone who is married knows the feeling. When I was dating my current spouse, I was willing to do about anything for her—and vice versa. If I wanted to climb a mountain, she was beside me. If I wanted to take a dip of Copenhagen, she would kiss me even with that nasty snuff in my mouth and love the taste. If I had just swallowed some tequila, she didn't mind. This is what happened with Christ. I didn't look at my new life as quitting drinking, but loving Christ and living the way He wanted me to live.

For example, I didn't quit dipping snuff, I loved Jesus. The cool part of eventually stopping is that God took away the craving to dip Copenhagen long before I quit. For a while, I still dipped at work, but at home or on vacation, I never cared about using tobacco. Eventually, after I finally completed my military service, I never touched it again. I had no craving to dip the stuff. God took this desire away long before I stopped.

Thanks to the faulty foundations from my childhood, my views of sexuality and all kinds of other stuff were messed up. Yet until I reached my mid-thirties, I didn't know that I desperately needed the foundation of faith in God. I never gave Him a chance. I never thought about the fallacy of the atheists who claimed there was no God but spent inordinate amounts of time trying to prove He didn't exist. Before I never asked one, "So if there is no

God, why do you hate him so much? Why do you spend all this time and energy trying to prove something you don't believe in?"

Learning the Truth

My outlook on life went through a profound shift in the weeks and months after I became a Christian. Instead of trying to justify ways that I could carry on with my old habits and still proclaim I believed in God, I no longer wanted to disappointment Him. Today, many people think there is no absolute truth, and that what is true for one person may not be true for another. The Bible says otherwise. Two plus two still equals four and always will, no matter how many people try to pretend it adds up to five. Truth is truth and sin is sin. The Bible tells me what is and isn't sin, and I don't get to choose words which I will follow and which I won't. I don't have a choice.

Just like all men or most men, we're still attracted to attractive women. If I found myself in a situation through temptation, I may be tempted, but I would need to stay faithful to the Lord and my wife and turn them away. I also have a natural inclination to anger, but I can choose to avoid giving in to my impulses or let my temper prod me to do something I will later regret. When Paul, the disciple who wrote about half of the books in the New Testament, chose a life of singleness, he didn't do it because he didn't like women or wasn't attracted to them. He wanted to honor God and do God's work.

So when it came to drinking, I saw that I had a choice. I used to love getting drunk. I could shed my inhibitions and laugh a lot (although the hangovers weren't much fun). But when I felt God tugging on my heart, I had to decide: Would I continue making a fool of myself because I liked the way liquor made me feel? Or should I honor Christ by staying sober? I'll never forget the day I read the verse: "And do not grieve the Holy Spirit of God, with whom you were sealed for the day of redemption" (Eph. 4:30). Until then, I never knew I grieved the Holy Spirit when I sinned. But it made sense. Now I recognized why I felt sad when I did something wrong. When the Spirit lived within me, I felt sad because He does. I hurt because He hurt.

None of this happened overnight. In fact, it took about four months before I realized this "Christian stuff" was working. One day I realized, "Wow, I've got all this extra money." I had to think it over, but it finally dawned on me. Because I wasn't blowing a small fortune every weekend on rum and tequila, I had a wad of cash in my wallet. Ironically, when we first joined the church, I told my wife, "I'm not going to change anything." (Even now, I can envision God chuckling, "Watch me.") Yet here I was, making changes right and left. Not because I had suddenly turned into a religious scholar. I just sensed God showing me the way I had been living was flat out wrong. Most of what I had done didn't violate Uncle Sam's laws, but it did God's.

Now, when it comes to what is right and wrong, a lot of people try to make things complex when they are not. Everyone knows it's against the law to commit murder. Many states used to frown on adultery, even permitting it as valid grounds for divorce. While many people no longer think sleeping around is any big deal, it violates God's moral law. Just as I shouldn't be unfaithful to my spouse, I shouldn't be stealing from my neighbor or coveting his new car, flat screen TV, or anything else he owns. I shouldn't be telling lies. It took me several years to stop digging Copenhagen, a habit I picked up in seventh grade with my first pinch on a golf course (by the time we reached third hole, I was sick). That didn't stop me from using it all the way through the military, but as the Holy Spirit gradually revealed biblical truths to me, I saw this stuff wasn't good for my body. And 1 Corinthians 3:17 says my body is a temple for the Holy Spirit.

Eternal Guidance

Imagine you have contracted a rare disease and your doctor has told you your illness is terminal. Six months at best. Suddenly the amount in your bank account, all those projects piling up at work, and the minutia that causes problems at home don't seem so important. You desperately want to devote time to passing on lessons to your children, who face the rest of their lives without your influence, advice, and guidance. When you try to talk to them, emotion clouds your mind and makes it nearly impossible to get anything out. That leaves communicating in writing. What are you going to tell them in your letter or e-mail? Will you share about some meaningless high school prank you pulled? Or your favorite TV show? Not likely. You will want to relate everything you know to help them live life to the fullest, keep them safe, and help them remain faithful and honorable. You will want to give them hope and a future. You might use some stories from your life that will help teach them, or an example from a friend's life that will drive home a point.

You will want to help them understand situations that they will face by relating some events that happened to you—along with some pointers about what you did right, or the mistakes you made that they should avoid. You will want to help them know what will happen if they choose a particular path. Why they should avoid drugs, since abusing them could mean ending up dead in a ditch somewhere. Why they should shun drinking alcohol to excess so they are drunk all the time, since that habit could mean winding up in jail, dead, or hurting somebody else. At the bare minimum, they could go broke. And how if they go out and have sex with every living creature they see, something bad is going to happen, whether they catch a sexually-transmitted disease or wind up with a broken heart.

If you did helped your children make wise choices and lead a fulfilling life, people who heard about what you did before your death would call you a caring parent. So why would we look at God's instructions any differently? This is what He did with the Bible. People (mainly those who never read it) often see it as a bunch of dusty old stories always warning, "Don't do this" or "don't do that." Wrong. God's Word is great stuff, packed with instruction and valuable insights for life. When you read it, it's as if God were standing in the room, giving you advice for life—which happens every time you read it.

Even some Christians fail to appreciate what an awesome gift Jesus gave us when He departed from this earth and sent the Holy Spirit to be our ever-present guide. In the Old Testament, the Spirit wasn't with God's children all the time. He would come and go. Sometimes, angels came down to talk to them. In the case of Moses, He showed up in a burning bush to offer direction. But He still wasn't with people every day. However, when Jesus left, the Holy Spirit came over Christ's followers on the day of Pentecost. Now, the Holy Spirit is in every person who believes in Jesus and the sacrifice He made. In fact, we get all three parts of God: Father, Son, and Holy Spirit.

Even though this is fantastic news, I gradually learned not everyone is happy about it.

In fact, it got to the point where I didn't want to tell anyone I was a Christian because it brought so many strange reactions, like I had sprouted horns from the top of my head. "Well, you probably don't like this or that," some would say. "You can't have any fun. You can't party or smoke dope anymore." Granted, they didn't understand a thing they were talking about. What upset me were all the Christians who seemed to care more about what denomination I belonged to, what Bible version I read, or how many times a week I prayed. Many seemed to want to be sure that I knew their views on scripture were superior to mine, as well as their church.

Part of the Same Body

After a while, I wondered if we had anything in common. Maybe more church members should do a tour of military duty. Whenever I traveled around the world, I quickly learned it didn't matter it I was white and my army buddy was an African-American. We were Americans, period. It didn't matter what country, what the circumstances were like, or what language the people there spoke. In Special Forces, I sometimes saw guys wearing "sterile" uniforms, meaning they had no Army insignia on them. When I asked why, they replied if they were captured, the enemy wouldn't know they were Americans. But sterile uniforms didn't hide our identity, just our unit. Everything branded us, whether our facial structure, the rucksack with "US" in bold letters, the M-4 rifles we carried, or the boots we wore. Everything said we were Americans, down to the odor we gave off.

This is the way I approach Christianity. Not as a member of the Assemblies of God, or a Baptist, a Lutheran, a Methodist, or an Episcopalian. As a Christian, I follow Christ. Still, many people pestered me until I would finally tell them—and add, "Okay? That's enough about denominations." One woman got mad at me for saying that because she belonged to a different denomination. I wondered if she thought I had herpes or could spread it like an airborne virus. If you believe that

- Christ was born of a virgin,
- lived a perfect life,
- died on the cross and shed His blood for the forgiveness of my sins,
- His resurrection makes a new life possible,
- Jesus is who He said He was and is God, that's all that matters. We're all part of the same body.

CHAPTER 7
The Foundation of Leadership

Once I discovered the foundation of faith, I found myself much better prepared to lead others. While there are numerous definitions of leadership and views on how to lead, the *Merriam-Webster Collegiate Dictionary* (eleventh edition) defines leadership as a position as a leader of a group or organization, or people who possess the power or ability to lead other people. I see leadership as the ability to influence others to reach a common goal. When it comes to Christian leadership, the goal is much higher. A Christian leader influences others to accomplish God's will in their life by motivating them and providing direction and vision. And at the same time, strengthening and improving His church.

Reflecting on what the Bible says about Christian leaders can be challenging, especially if we apply its standards to leaders of today. One of the chief passages addressing leadership appears in 1 Timothy: "Here is a trustworthy saying: Whoever aspires to be an overseer desires a noble task. Now the overseer is to be above reproach, faithful to his wife, temperate, self-controlled, respectable, hospitable, able to teach, not given to drunkenness, not violent but gentle, not quarrelsome, not a lover of money. He must manage his own family well and see that his children obey him, and he must do so in a manner worthy of full respect. (If anyone does not know how to manage his own family, how can he take care of God's church?) He must not be a recent convert, or he may become conceited and fall under the same judgment as the devil. He must also have a good reputation with outsiders, so that he will not fall into disgrace and into the devil's trap" (1 Timothy 3:1–7, NIV).

As I look around American society, I wonder how many people meet these requirements. How many pastors do you know who are unable to keep their children in line? Whose kids make you wonder how they were raised? I know one pastor's children who are wild and unruly. If I didn't know their father was a pastor, I would never have guessed they come from a Christian family, let alone are the children of a pastor. I know another family where the pastor's children have picked up the arrogance he projects to almost everyone around him. (Personally, I never understood pride or arrogance, at least not since I made a decision to follow Christ and saw all my accomplishments as secondary to His.)

Qualities of Leadership

These kinds of displays in a church environment sadden me because I expect better from people who claim to follow Christ. Arrogant Christians remind me of my days in Special Forces. Often, when new guys joined the First Special Forces Group Airborne group as qualified Green Berets, their heads swelled with so much pride they had to turn sideways to get through the doorway into the team room. I would ask many, "Why do you think you're so special?" Then I would inform them that we appreciated the fact they had just completed a very difficult course and were deserving of their accolades. Indeed, we needed their help with the United States's strategic mission.

Yet as much as we enhanced the military's capabilities, I advised them that despite their visions of grandeur, our group did not win wars single-handedly. We didn't even supply ourselves with basics, like ammunition. We needed all the cooks because without them we would not get our food. We needed the supply sergeants; without them we would not get the supplies we desperately needed to accomplish our missions. The United States wins wars with numerous elements, such as infantry soldiers, tankers, pilots, Marines, and sailors, as well as supply sergeants, ammo sergeants, and cooks. "Yes, you have accomplished something that most people have not," I would conclude. "But don't ever think of yourself as the only ones who win the war. Be humble. You will need help someday of all these people around you."

When it comes to leadership, the first quality a person must embrace is humility. Moses is one of the most outstanding examples of this kind of leader. When God came to him in the middle of the desert and told him, "So now, go. I am sending you to Pharaoh to bring my people the Israelites out of Egypt," Moses's reaction was: "Who am I that I should go to Pharaoh and bring the Israelites out of Egypt?" (Ex. 3:10–11). *Who am I?* No matter how awesome or seemingly mundane the task or responsibility, when God calls a person to do something, a humble person will feel challenged and possibly overwhelmed. He or she won't assume they are so great they are a natural selection for the job. Instead, people who possess humility will follow the advice Paul gave to the church at Rome: "For by the grace given me I say to every one of you: Do not think of yourself more highly than you ought, but rather think of yourself with sober judgment, in accordance with the faith

God has distributed to each of you. For just as each of us has one body with many members, and these members do not all have the same function, so in Christ we, though many, form one body, and each member belongs to all the others" (Rom. 12:3–5, NIV).

Finding Fault

As I contemplate that pastor with unruly children or the one I see as arrogant, I may have been too hard on both of them. If we look hard enough, we can all find fault with each other. Unfortunately, we sometimes harbor expectations for Christians that are much too high, especially when it comes to pastors and their families. It can be a daunting (even impossible) task for some Christians who aspire to leadership within the church, because of how others' views them, or even their own wounded self-image. Regardless of where you stand in your leadership aspirations—whether as a Bible study or small group leader, elder, or pastor—the Bible teaches that leaders are appointed by God: "Let everyone be subject to the governing authorities, for there is no authority except that which God has established. The authorities that exist have been established by God" (Rom. 13:1, NIV).

If any of you reading these words aspire to church leadership, I want to give you some hope. Christ chose Paul to be a leader, God chose David to be king, and God chose Moses to lead Israel out of captivity in Egypt, a story so powerful it is known thousands of years later by a simple term: "The Exodus." Yet each of these men had great flaws and personal struggles with sin. Each would have fallen short of meeting all the qualifications listed in 1 Timothy. Before Jesus changed his life, Paul was a chief persecutor of Christians, setting out to round up believers in Damascus the way he had hounded—even killed—Christ's followers in Jerusalem. David committed adultery with Bathsheba and then compounded his sin by sending her husband to his death. Moses's murder of an Egyptian was the reason he fled from Egypt and wound up in the desert in the first place.

To briefly recount their stories:

- Paul

    "Meanwhile, Saul was still breathing out murderous threats against the Lord's disciples. He went to the high priest and asked him for letters to the synagogues in Damascus, so that if he found any there who belonged to the Way, whether men or women, he might take them as prisoners to Jerusalem. As he neared Damascus on his journey, suddenly a light from heaven flashed around him. He fell to the ground and heard a voice say to him, 'Saul, Saul, why do you persecute me?' 'Who are you, Lord?' Saul asked. 'I am Jesus, whom you are persecuting,' he replied. 'Now get up and go into the city, and you will be told what you must do'" (Acts 9:1–6).

- David
 "One evening David got up from his bed and walked around on the roof of the palace.
 From the roof he saw a woman bathing. The woman was very beautiful, and David sent someone to find out about her. The man said, 'She is Bathsheba, the daughter of Eliam and the wife of Uriah the Hittite.' Then David sent messengers to get her. She came to him, and he slept with her. (Now she was purifying herself from her monthly uncleanness.) Then she went back home. The woman conceived and sent word to David, saying, 'I am pregnant.'... In the morning David wrote a letter to Joab and sent it with Uriah. In it he wrote, 'Put Uriah out in front where the fighting is fiercest. Then withdraw from him so he will be struck down and die'" (2 Sam. 11:2–5 and 14–15, NIV).

- Moses
 "One day, after Moses had grown up, he went out to where his own people were and watched them at their hard labor. He saw an Egyptian beating a Hebrew, one of his own people. Looking this way and that and seeing no one, he killed the Egyptian and hid him in the sand" (Ex. 2:11–12, NIV).

Choosing Leaders

There are many other examples of God choosing leaders who wouldn't withstand careful examination by a church board or deacon committee. We wouldn't select them no matter what kind of scriptural examples we could read about God picking the unlikeliest of leaders. Had I been a member of my current congregation, I probably wouldn't have voted for myself as lead pastor. I brought some serious baggage to the position. Not only was I divorced, in my early days as a believer, I struggled with a quick temper, self-centeredness, and fondness for alcohol. Granted, by the time God called me to the ministry, I no longer got drunk, had brought my temper under control, and with Christ's help, had learned to love others as much as myself. Even though not a Christian at the time of my divorce, I still had that blemish on my record. Indeed, I had no idea why God would choose a man like me. I did not feel worthy to be one of His leaders. That is, until He showed me the full impact of stories of men like Paul, David, and Moses.

If they could do God's work, so could I. I still find it hard to believe that a former Green Beret can be a preacher. My wife does not like it when I say this, but it is true: The government spent millions of dollars teaching me to eliminate key targets for them (taking lives) and God spent nothing teaching me how to save lives (leading people to Christ). Yet my story is no more amazing than many others I have heard in recent years. Everyone who makes the decision to follow Jesus has an inspiring story to share.

When we look at the word *authority*, most people's thoughts turn first to government. Church members will also think of their pastor, deacons, or elders. However, most of us are in some kind of authority or leadership. Even if you oversee just one person at your place of work, you are a leader. If you are married, you lead your family. You also lead your own life (a bit of a stretch for this topic, but still true). If single, you lead yourself morally by staying pure for your future spouse. You are also the leader of your relationship with God, which comes through reading His Word, fellowshipping with other Christians, and prayer. Do you lead yourself through God's word or your own philosophy? If you aspire to be a leader and can't lead yourself properly, how do you expect to lead anyone else?

In our lives we all struggle to accomplish our goals, some more than others. To accomplish anything worthwhile requires effort and risk. While effort will help you accomplish your goal, risk is the scary one. Whenever we take a risk, that includes the inherent chance that we will fail. Legendary inventor Thomas Edison once said, "I have not failed. I've just found 10,000 ways that won't work."[1] One of my favorite quotes on this topic is attributed to Elbert Hubbard (1856–1915), an editor, publisher, and writer who commented, "There is no failure except in no longer trying."[2]

I say that recognizing that these kinds of statements would ring hollow to someone whose business just collapsed, or who failed to get the grades needed to stay in medical school. They tried, but they did not accomplish their goals. In their eyes, they failed. However, I have lived long enough to know we all experience highs and lows in our lives. Peaks and valleys are a normal part of human existence. Everyone—or least the people I have known—has had ups and downs for a little while. That may be for a week or a month. In some cases, the struggles go on for years. This can relate to our ineffective leadership of ourselves. Sometimes, all you need is a vacation to recharge your batteries or insights from a leadership conference to help you get back on track.

Leading Ourselves

If most of us take an honest and penetrating look at self, we will reach the conclusion that we need to start leading ourselves better. We need to stay focused, set goals, have accountability partners in our lives, and establish better plans of what we want to do. When I served with Special Forces, we always drew up plans for our missions called Special Forces Brief Back; they were more involved and extensive than the "operations order" that most other army units followed when planning their combat missions. The operations order included the situation, mission, and activities needed to reach the combat mission's goal. However, the Special Forces Brief Back plan had to go into extensive detail and map out a primary, alternate, contingency, and emergency plan for every potential scenario. If we were parachuting into an area, we had to outline four drop zones in case we couldn't jump into the first drop zone, or even the first two alternatives.

That may sound extreme; some people would sneer military operatives must suffer from an obsessive-compulsive disorder. Yet with life often throwing a monkey wrench in your plan A, how prepared are you to adjust and follow plan B (or C or D)? Say you plan to be an engineer and want to enroll in a prestigious university. For example, your dream school is Yale. However, when you submit your application, they reject it. Crestfallen by this unexpected turn of events, you give up and say, "Well, since my no. 1 choice said no, I guess I will no longer plan to be an engineer. Instead, I'll go drive a school bus." Really? Because life interrupted your dream, you're ready to quit on it? Therefore, you must consider more than one option in life or more than one way to accomplish your goal. Most people with aspirations for higher learning apply to several schools, figuring they will select from the ones that accept them. Likewise, how many plans do you have to accomplish you calling in life? Take a moment and evaluate what you want to be in your life, what has God called you to be, and whether the two complement each other.

This can be a very difficult decision, especially if you have already established yourself in a career and then decided to follow Christ. Indeed, it can be disconcerting if you sense the Holy Spirit saying that God wants you to quit your job, become a full-time missionary, and move overseas (granted, that sounds extreme, but it has happened to some people). I have a friend who recently quit a high-paying job as an aerospace engineer; he designed engines for rocket ships. Yet when God called him to ministry just shy of his mid-fifties, he responded. He won't be able to draw any retirement pay, and then not full benefits, until the next decade. Considering what he walked away from, this represented a monumental decision.

Large or small, good or bad, every decision we make can have a dramatic impact on the future. So before making a move, just consider the impact a particular decision can make on your life and how frightening this decision can be! It was for me! In December of 2010, I heard God's still, small voice calling me to the ministry. This definitely was not my plan. Still on active duty, I had served eighteen years of active duty service in the United States Army and had only two years to reaching full retirement benefits (total time in the Army and Army Reserves was about twenty-two years). My plans were to attending a university and earning my master's degree in business (MBA). This would also take about two years. Once I completed my MBA and twenty years of active service, I would be ready for my next chapter in life.

In my mind, my ideal plan involved retiring from the Army and joining the corporate world after applying for jobs in the Seattle-Tacoma area in my home state of Washington. My ideal daydream included receiving an offer I could not refuse. I would land in a plush office on the forty-fifth floor of a skyscraper overlooking Puget Sound in downtown Seattle. Obviously, this was not God's plan for me after retirement. Instead of studying for an MBA, I switched gears and enrolled in a Christian university to complete a master's degree in ministry. I also had to make a major mental adjustment to accept a much lower salary than I had once envisioned. Indeed, God's call to become a pastor has been a challenge ever since He revealed His plans. Some people think pastors only work on Sundays, but only because they don't see all the counseling, prayer, Bible study, and countless other details that are part of this position.

Wise Decisions

While most of you reading these words likely don't fit into the mold of a pastor, God calls every one of His children to some type of ministry. We are to expand His kingdom and, in the process, bring glory to Him. Many Christians struggle with their calling and what to do with it. I've seen two points of views about this calling. Both are a little unbalanced. The first is that God will provide everything and it's all up to Him. The other is that we are all called and we must do it ourselves. Here is where you need a balanced perspective to appreciate that it is some of both. God calls us and guides us, and yet we must decide what to do with God's directions. I understand that God can do anything He wants. He can supernaturally interject what job we do with the path we take.

However, this is not the norm. He has always involved humans to do His work for Him. Moses had to walk to Egypt, confront Ramesses, wade through constant opposition, and overcome the doubts of his own people to lead the Israelites out of Egypt. Abraham had to follow through with Sarah in order to get her pregnant when was seemingly too old to bear a child. The young shepherd boy, David, had to take the challenge to stand up against nine-foot-tall Goliath. More often than not, God wants us to take on the responsibility for our own decisions, good and bad. We can look at many biblical examples to see how everyday decision-making was a part of life for God's leaders:

- After all this had happened, *Paul decided* to go to Jerusalem, passing through Macedonia and Achaia. "After I have been there," he said, "I must visit Rome also" (Acts 19:21, NIV, emphasis added).
- *Paul had decided* to sail past Ephesus to avoid spending time in the province of Asia, for he was in a hurry to reach Jerusalem, if possible, by the day of Pentecost (Acts 20:16, NIV, emphasis added).
- They served as judges for the people at all times. The difficult cases they brought to Moses, but the simple ones they *decided themselves* (Exodus 18:26, NIV, emphasis added).

All of us need to make decisions every day, some more important than others. However, a Christian's ability to do this is a critical skill to possess for life and fulfilling God's ministry plan for you. As we grow in Christ, we should have a good track record of making wise, biblical decisions as evidence of spiritual growth. Indeed, we should seek God first in every major decision we face. This involves prayer, seeking wisely counsel, and studying God's Word, the Bible. First Thessalonians 5:17 (ESV) tells us to "pray without ceasing." Proverbs 15:22 (NIV) advises, "Plans fail for lack of counsel, but with many advisers they succeed." Paul wrote to Timothy, "All Scripture is God-breathed and is useful for teaching, rebuking, correcting and training in righteousness, so that the servant of God may be thoroughly equipped for every good work" (2 Tim. 3:16–17, NIV).

Taking Action

In my life, God has typically used prayer as the initial way He instructs me in making decisions, and action that should follow. Through prayer He called me into ministry, led me to the church I now serve, and continues to lead me throughout numerous aspects of life. We should always trust God and commit our decisions to God through prayer. If we commit to do what God has for us, we should have peace of mind that everything will be okay. As Jeremiah 29:11 teaches, God plans to prosper us, not harm us, and give us a hope and a future.

After I pray and receive guidance from God, I will seek counsel from wise leaders, starting with my wife. I also seek to discern God's will by studying scripture. I don't mean to imply that every decision you face requires outside counsel, but when you are dealing with issues of major concern, it is wise to ask for others' insights and advice. When I sensed God leading me to move our church to a new location, I sought counsel from others whose wisdom and Bible knowledge I respected. As Proverbs 15:22 (NIV) says, "Plans fail for lack of counsel, but with many advisers they succeed." However, when I needed a new printer for my computer, I made that decision.

Godly Christians can often contribute to helping us reach important decisions by introducing new perspectives or insights that we had not considered, help with questions we may have, and confirm whether the decision we are contemplating is a wise choice. However, be cautious with who you choose for counselors. Seek advice from someone who will be open and honest, not someone who will "go along with the crowd" or simply tell you what you want to hear because they are afraid of your reaction if they don't "go along to get along."

Finally, seek what the Bible says about the situation. Search for scriptures that may apply to your situation, check cross-references, study them further, and evaluate this wisdom as you strive to reach a sound decision. Once you have prayed, sought wise counsel, and studied what God has to say, you must act—trusting that God will lead you, provide what you need as you move forward, and that His will indeed will be done in your life.

However, don't allow yourself to get so "spiritual" or afraid of making the wrong move that you never act. Understand that even though God will show you what He wants, it is still up to you to follow His calling. I have seen people who allow their lack of trust in the Lord keep themselves from ever making a decision. A man I know said he sensed God calling him into ministry nearly twenty years ago. Though everything seemed to proceed well with the training he pursued with his pastor at the time, when that man departed, the new pastor had no interest in helping him grow (which is why about twenty people departed from that church. They were then able to do what they felt God calling them to do, with the help of other leaders). Yet this man remained in place, even after his current pastor ordered books for a new training course, but never followed through to set up the classes. Finally, I asked how much progress he had made the first three years after he felt a call to ministry. After this man said it had been great, I then asked how much progress he made since that pastor came fourteen years ago, he admitted he had been standing still ever since. I said, "God wants us to walk through life doing things for Him, but it's up to you to act. If your pastor is hindering your ability to do that, I would question if you should stay at that church." We read in James 1:23–25, "For if anyone is a hearer of the word and not a doer, he is like a man who looks intently at his natural face in a mirror. For he looks at himself and goes away and at once forgets what he was like. But the one who looks into the perfect law, the law of liberty, and perseveres, being no hearer who forgets but a doer who acts, he will be blessed in his doing."

This kind of indecisiveness can paralyze churches, too. I heard about a church that had been searching for a pastor since early in 2011. More than three years later, they were still getting by with interim pastors, traveling speakers, and other stop-gap solutions. One day, I asked a guy who attends the church why they had never filled their pulpit. "Well," he said, "the leaders cannot agree on who they should hire. They have to have a unanimous decision and no one can agree on anything, and nobody wants to force a decision, so they keep going without a pastor."

That may sound silly, even ludicrous. Yet how many people reading these words have followed a similar "kick the can" philosophy in life, failing to ever break out of the familiar rut where they live? It won't be enough to decide to do so. Action must follow if you expect to fulfill the plans God has for your life.

Notes

1. Goodreads, http://www.goodreads.com/quotes/tag/failure.
2. "Elbert Hubbard Quotes," ThinkExist.com, http://thinkexist.com/quotation/there_is_no_failure_except_in_no_longer_trying

CHAPTER 8
The Foundation of Positive Speech

The words that so many people tossed at me in my childhood stung like a scorpion. Not just the infamous "retard" label, but the putdowns that questioned my integrity, family heritage, or chances of ever succeeding in life. I wondered how people could be so cruel, especially adults who ought to have understood the tender spirit of a young child and how quickly I would take those words to heart.

As bad as it was when I grew up, I think modern influences have made it even worse. Take the online anonymity that allows people to attack others with no regard for decency or the damage their words inflict. Or the polarized political climate that spills over into so many other areas of life. Or simply the natural human inclination to focus on the bad, a habit that spreads virally through modern communication devices. It adds up to a society brimming with negative speech, and hurling such messages at young people as "You'll never amount to anything," "You'll never get that done," or "You'll never have enough money to go to college, so don't bother."

These negative speech patterns originate in the home. Take a young father I know, I regularly hear him tell his child things like, "No, no, no, no, put that down. Put that away. Stop doing that. Don't touch that. If you don't listen to me, these are the consequences." Aside from the continual stream of negativity, this father compounds the problem by never following through and delivering any consequences (a sign of the need for discipline, which I reviewed in chapter 5).

This reminds me of the news report I heard once about societal problems created by young children growing up in a similar manner. Namely, constantly hearing "no" from their parents, but never experiencing any follow-through. Their parent either gives in or makes compromise, whether it's giving the child a smaller toy than they asked for, or a different type of candy, or letting them watch a TV program after proclaiming they couldn't.

However, the parent who tells their son or daughter, "No, you cannot have that" but fails to stand strong when they keep asking reaps a bitter harvest. As a youngster matures and starts to interact with other children and adults and later develops dating relationships, they take their earlier lessons into account. Over time, they have learned that "no" just means they must ask again, ask differently, try harder, or make some kind of compromise to get what they want.

While you may not immediately make the connection, continuously telling your child "no, no, no" without following through is a form of negative speech. Why? Because it fails to make a positive impact on their foundation. If you tell a child "no," you must stand your ground. The Bible teaches us to raise up our child in the way they should go. Train up a child in the way he should go; even when he is old he will not depart from it (Prov. 22:6, ESV). When children are obedient, celebrate with them. Tell them why you are pleased and what positive lesson they have just learned. Positive speech is a blessing. Unlike the kind so common in our world, it is telling someone— whether your child, another kid, or even a co-worker: "You can do this."

Lining Up with Truth

Words of affirmation must line up with the truth of scripture. A pastor hoping to inspire an otherwise-apathetic congregation may tell them that, in the words of Philippians 4:13, they can do all things through Christ who strengthens them. While that is true, what that passage is talking about is doing something to honor God, such as turning your back on your old habits and ways in order to follow a new path. In such cases, Jesus gives us the strength to overcome those old temptations.

However, it does not mean that you can do anything you can imagine. Someone might want to be a professional basketball player, but if they measure five feet, seven inches tall and have a vertical leap of two inches, their chances of making it to the pros are pretty slim. So how can we make this situation positive? What do we tell the child whose chance of becoming a professional basketball player does not even rate, one in a million? Encourage him or her to simply do their best. What if they will never play professionally? Just because a child isn't great at physically playing a sport, it does not mean that they cannot participate in that sport. Countless numbers of professional coaches, trainers, and medical personnel did not play professional basketball, but they have much to offer the sport.

If you are in a position to train or mentor a young person, your goal should be to help them learn to play their favorite sport and teach them to do the best they possibly can. Keep in mind that all the time you will be helping reinforcing the idea that their efforts are valuable and that learning whatever game it happens to be, will benefit them in more ways than just staying in shape and having fun. For example, as that young person continues to play, you may see that they're not likely to make the varsity, let alone be a superstar. They may get quite frustrated as their dreams collide with reality. However, as you teach that young person, you can impart lessons about sportsmanship, teamwork, and the valuable role every person plays on a team. You can say, "Well, you may not be the star player, but you can help other players improve their skills, understand the game, and help the team win a championship."

As we raise our children, we must always be aware of the foundation we are laying. Many people have obstacles in their life, but learn to work around them. Those obstacles may be the very thing that help them to work harder and enhance their eventual success in life. One of the biggest mistakes we can make is thinking that everyone should have a smooth path with no disappointments, setbacks, or hard knocks along the way. So if you're dealing with a child from an underprivileged background, don't pity them. Help them to learn and overcome their challenges with the value of positive speech.

Ability to Learn

As I have mentioned previously, not everybody learns the same way, but we all have the ability to learn. Remember that as you work with a child, whether yours or someone else's, the foundation of positive speech can create positive outcomes. In the same way, negative speech can shipwreck their life. If all a child hears is negative speech, their outlook on life can quickly turn negative. When a parent comes home from work and their conversation revolves around how miserable they are at their job, how crummy their salary is, or how stupid their boss or co-workers are, they are helping their child create a faulty foundation.

This is serious, because it instills a negative outlook in the child. As they prepare to go into the world, it dims their expectations of the future. They are already developing the idea that they won't like their job and life will be full of drudgery. Equally bad is how this pattern is likely to repeat itself as they later sow the same pattern of negative speech into their children.

After all, speech starts with the way we think. I remember in my younger years of performing martial arts, when a coach would tell me I had the ability to defeat an opponent. He would teach me to go home and put positive sticky notes all over the bathroom mirror, so I would see them in the morning as I shaved and got ready for the day. He would cram my head with other positive reinforcement, creating the kind of foundation that sent me into the match with the confidence that I would emerge victorious.

Every morning when I woke up and went to the bathroom to brush my teeth, shave, and comb my hair, I would see reminders that I could win this fight because I was better trained than my opponent. That I worked harder and was faster and more skilled. I didn't just have little sticky notes all up and down the mirrors either. I left them around my bedroom and on the steering wheel of my car. Now, this didn't mean that I was victorious in every match. I wasn't the best in the world (not even my state), nor did I become a professional fighter. Still, this training was part of a positive foundation that helped me succeed later in life. Whenever I did something, I did it with all my heart and energy and with a positive attitude. I felt that I could not fail.

For instance, take the time I decided to attend Special Forces selection (better known as the Green Berets). By this point in my army career, I had already qualified as an airborne infantryman, a sniper, a Ranger, and was a combat veteran. Yet when I told people I planned to try out for Special Forces, many replied, "Well, you won't make it." Since most of those people were either in my chain of command or outranked me, I didn't react in a hostile way. But several times I declared, "Well, I'm not worried about failing. I only want to know if I will be number one or number two." Often, I thought to myself, "They must have tried and failed, or they were too scared to even try."

Those naysayers didn't defeat me. First, in my mind I had already made it. I set my goals and I knew I would attain them; I had no doubt. Selection has no ranking process, I never discovered whether I made that number one or two ranking, but I did make it. Once I completed selection, it was off to the Q course, the qualification course for Special Forces, this is where we learned our job. My success in the military stemmed from a positive foundation that was laid years before.

Building the Foundation

My foundation did not originate with my coaches; it started with my mother. In spite of all the chaos, dysfunction, and challenges that I faced growing up, she helped create a positive foundation through her constant encouragement.

Although she understood the academic challenges I faced, she assured me that I could do anything I set my mind to accomplish. She often said things like "You might have to study harder than everybody else, but you have the ability to learn, just like they do. Don't get discouraged because it takes you longer to learn."

Those words became a self-fulfilling prophecy. The underpinning she helped establish when I was a young child keeps me going to this day. It was especially valuable when I entered Special Forces, which was much more difficult, academically, than typical Army training. During this specialized schooling, there were many times when my friends and other peers were out on the town having a good time, and I had to stay back in the barracks so I could study for an exam. Or write my portion of the mission plan (brief back operations plan). But in the end, I walked across that graduation stage with everyone else.

Nor did the impact of my mother's words stop with my military achievements. Her positive words were especially valuable my first year in college. I felt terrified over not having the intelligence or intellectual ability to even be there. Yet Mom's words kept echoing through my mind: "You may have to study harder than others around you, but you will learn. You can do it." And I did. A kid once called a retard, labeled too slow and too dumb to do much in life, now holds a bachelor's degree in business administration, a master's degree in ministry, and a master's degree in leadership. I'm not more intelligent than anyone else out there, nor any smarter. I just had a foundation laid that taught me that I can do whatever I set my mind to do. As I soon head into my fifth decade of life, I have not quit speaking words. Positive speech will be a part of me until the day I die.

After all, God doesn't tell us, "You can do nothing through Christ" or "You are a failure." He tells us we can do all things through Christ. As we read the Bible or hear a pastor preach the Word of God, God is giving us positive speech, a hope for the future despite our circumstances. One of my favorite passages in the Bible comes from Jeremiah 29:10–13, right after the prophet has told Israel they will spend seventy years in captivity in Babylon. Then Jeremiah follows with these hopeful words from God: "'I will visit you and perform My good word toward you, and cause you to return to this place. For I know the thoughts that I think toward you, says the LORD, thoughts of peace and not of evil, to give you a future and a hope. Then you will call upon Me and go and pray to Me, and I will listen to you. And you will seek Me and find Me, when you search for Me with all your heart.'"

It is crucial to meditate on such promises. As we read the Word of God, we hear it in our minds. As we hear the words of God speaking to us, His speech becomes part of our foundation—our spiritual DNA so to speak. Through this we become positive people, whose speech becomes life. Not only to ourselves, but to others. Yes, I know the economy has been bad for a long time. Yes, I know the world is experiencing earth-shaking upheaval. Yes, I know that nothing is like it used to be. But because I have a relationship with God who sees all, knows all, and meets our needs, I know that I don't need to be caught up in the negative chorus that typifies modern-day America.

Influencing Our Children

As parents raising our children, we are the primary influence on their foundation. Ironically, today we live in a culture that likes to proclaim that everyone's a winner, and there are no losers. Not only is this false, as soon as families get on the playground and the competition starts, the idea there are no losers quickly falls by the wayside. Everyone wants to celebrate a victory because they scored the most runs, or goals, or touchdowns. As we gather up the little kiddos and put them in their twelve-point safety harnesses in the back seats, surrounded by fifteen air bags to protect them from danger, we want to tell them that they outscored the other team and really did win.

While we may like to think this is positive speech, the question is, what do you say when they lose? What happens when the other team scores more points? Don't think that your children are too dumb to understand or recognize that there is an inherent contradiction in telling them they were winners last week because they scored more touchdowns, but this week they are still supposedly winners when the other team scored more touchdowns. Maintaining a positive attitude toward your children, no matter whether they win or lose, creates the kind of foundation of success and achievement that you as a parent want them to have.

Too often parents get in the car and blame their children's loss on the referees, the coach, or the other players. Some may even berate their own children for their "dumb" mistakes. It still makes me cringe to think that parents engage in the same kind of behavior some of my teachers did, but I know it happens. Getting into that car and telling your child that if they just had better referees, or griping that they made all the calls in favor of the other team, doesn't do a thing to build a positive foundation in a child. Always blaming someone else for losses is not helping learn responsibility for what they've done. It doesn't help them learn how to talk to other players, and in the case of referees, it can sour their attitude towards all kinds of authority. Tell them, "That other team played very well today. But so did your team and I'm proud of you. It's not every day you can win, but if you always give your best and support your team with your best, there will always be a positive outcome in life."

You can also give them a "for instance." Since I live in Washington, I love to use the Seattle Seahawks as an example a team that makes a great impact on its community and state. In 2015, everyone in our region was disappointed when the Seahawks fell one yard short of winning the Super Bowl. We were even more disappointed when their valiant comeback in the following season's divisional playoff game against Carolina came up one touchdown shy. Yet while they may not win every game, every time the Seahawks step on that field, they give 110 percent. They play the best they can on that particular day to support their team, their family, and the community.

Responding to Disappointment

Life is full of challenges. The difference in succeeding is not constantly reveling in the victories, but how we respond when we make mistakes. It's all about whether we get up again to play another game after we lose. Using positive speech to mold your child's character helps lay a valuable foundation. Whether good or bad, the lessons we are teaching them today get buried deep into their spirit. How we speak to them now will influence them for the rest of their lives.

When it comes to establishing a foundation for your children or a youngster you are mentoring, God's Word offers valuable guidance. One example of the need for positive speech appears in Paul's letter to Timothy: "Let no one despise you for your youth, but set the believers an example in speech, in conduct, in love, in faith, in purity" (1 Tim. 4:12, ESV). Another is found in Paul's letter to Titus: "Show yourself in all respects to be a model of good works, and in your teaching show integrity, dignity, and sound speech that cannot be condemned, so that an opponent may be put to shame, having nothing evil to say about us" (Titus 2:7–8, ESV).

As parents, we should model our actions on these scriptures as we teach our children and other young people integrity, dignity, and sound speech. The way we speak to children is crucial.

As a parent, I have endured the discipline wars. I know what it feels like to repeat myself a thousand times with the lesson seeming to never sink in. I know how easy it is to lose your temper and blurt out intemperate words or empty threats. Still, successful parenting means accepting the challenge and teaching kids to speak properly and use positive words in everything they do. Words are powerful. The first two chapters of Genesis describe God speaking the world into existence. He created the universe through His words. What we say, and how we say it, matters. Be the influence and lay the foundation for your children and their future children.

Presently you may be thinking; "Well, I wasn't raised in that kind of nurturing environment. How can I change?" Change happens within. Start small. Don't expect your foundation to be perfect if it sprang up from faulty guidance and negative speech. One of the things that we must understand as adults is that we can only effect change in ourselves. If we want our children to imitate our actions, we must be the example we expect them to follow. The legendary "Serenity Prayer," which has been adopted by Alcoholics Anonymous and other twelve-step programs (and is credited to several authors) says, "God, grant me the serenity to accept the things I cannot change, courage to change the things I can, and wisdom to know the difference." This prayer is a good example of how we should approach a foundational change as adults. No one is perfect; we all are a work in progress. However, the progress that we are working on should be a positive and not a negative.

Making an Impact

Most of us know people from our high school days and how some have moved past youthful cliques and "in crowd" status to become successful in their chosen careers. Today they are making a positive impact on society. Then there are others who, because of their negative choices, have wandered so far off track that high school represents the best times. If the latter resembles your story, it is never too late to change. Start by making small choices. For example, when you get up in the morning, say something to yourself that is positive. Set a small goal such as "Today, I will only tell my children positive words. When they do something wrong, I will express to them why positive actions are better than negative ones."

If you're asking yourself, "Well, Mr. Smart Guy, how can I do this?" the example I would give is one I lived. Say your child goes into the kitchen, opens a gallon of milk, and while trying to pour a glass, succeeds in spilling milk all over the floor. More than once in such circumstances I would gripe, "Why did you make such a big mess? Who's going to clean this up?" I had to learn that sort of emotional eruption helped build a negative foundation. Your goal is to teach them that what they did was not a good thing.

Instead of getting mad at them for doing the same thing you did as a child, you could say, "I remember when I spilled milk. It happens. You know what I did? I cleaned it up and then asked for help to pour my next glass because the milk jug was too heavy for me." As your child cleans up the spill, praise them for doing such a good job. Then offer to help them pour the next glass: "I know the jug is too heavy, so let's do this together. You hold the glass while I pour the milk." Once you've done that, you can point out how much easier things go when you work together as a team. Remind them the next time they need a glass of milk or juice to ask for help so you can act as a team again.

While this is a small, seemingly trifling example, it is only one of many ways that you can use the power of positive speech to lay a foundation in your child's life. Teach them the power of words coupled with positive action. In the same way God created the world with words, what we speak will also lead to action. Laying the foundation of positive speech does not happen overnight, especially if you lacked a properly-developed one growing up. Still, each and every one of us wants the best for ourselves and our loved ones. Even if you suffer the drawbacks of a negative foundation in life, that doesn't mean you have to remain stuck there.

Start small. Put sticky notes on your mirror as you get ready in the morning —and later, reminders on your computer or smartphone. Write affirming messages with positive words, such as, "I will demonstrate love today," "I will praise someone else today," "The words I speak have power and the power that I want to speak is love." Start by changing yourself. As you change, others around you will change. If you have children, the positive foundation that you plan for yourself will also be laid for them.

I also suggest you open your Bible and start regularly reading and meditating on God's Word. God loves you; He only wants the best for you and your family. Everyone endures struggles, which reflects the truth of Christ's promise: "In this world you will have trouble. But take heart! I have overcome the world" (John 16:33). Despite our troubles, this promise can help us adopt a positive outlook. Namely, that *we will* make it through the struggles. We can either adopt that outlook or allow the struggles to defeat and discourage us. Pray for God to give you the strength that you desire and the wisdom that you need to make it. Start laying a new foundation if you need to and remember the one that you are creating for your children can launch them toward success.

CHAPTER 9
The Foundation of Goal Setting

I'm not a big guy. When I was in the infantry, I weighed 165 pounds and stood five-foot-nine. I know I was not a small guy, little average. But when you're carrying eighty to ninety pounds on your back, you're a runt. There's nothing worse than being a relative runt when your commanding officer barks out the order, "All right, troops! Prepare for a twenty-mile road march!" Now, you may consider that just part of Army life. But you must consider that these long-range road marches included carrying the weight of a combat load, a weapon, and our rucksack (backpack), which all together frequently weighed more than one hundred pounds. That represented nearly two-thirds of my body weight.

Sound impossible? The secret of making it was; I never walked twenty miles. I always broke it down into smaller and smaller chunks. Whenever we broke ranks and started down the road, I would pick out a spot a mile away and march to that spot. Then I would pick out another intersection a mile or two in the distance. By the end of the march, my body sagging from the heavy load, I moved my mark from telephone pole to telephone pole. The only way I survived these grueling ordeals was setting smaller, attainable goals.

One of the biggest drawbacks for millions of people is their failure to set goals. Without any goals in mind, we will fail to draw up any plans to reach them. The ultimate effect is drifting through life, never going anywhere or accomplishing much. The point isn't that everyone has to become a nationally-known leader, a world-famous inventor, or the CEO. An average couple who raise well-adjusted children and contribute to the well-being of their community are just as much a success as someone who achieves great fame. And somewhere along the way, those "ordinary" people likely set some goals—for themselves and their children.

Most of us set goals, although we often don't think of them as such. We have a goal to see a popular movie, go on a vacation, finish this special-interest class, or to get married. Once we set these goals, we establish a plan, asking ourselves, "How are we going to do this? How are we going to get from point A to point B?" When you set out to buy a car, you have a goal in mind. It may be to find a reasonably-priced model to lower your monthly payments. Or find more reliable transportation. But many never stop to think about a plan for how to pay it off. Yes, we may check our budget before going to get a loan, when the bank establishes a plan for us. Over so many years, if we make the payments, we will hold the title to the car instead of the bank.

While we set numerous goals for things like movies and cars, we often fail to set a goal for our own lives and the success we seek. However, it isn't enough to set a goal. You also have to make plans for how to achieve them. After all, you can establish a goal like having a new job, a bigger house, finishing college, or obtaining a graduate degree. Next you need an intended path to get there. We can never reach our goal without a plan. Likewise, we can never have a plan without a goal. Consequently, goals and plans co-exist and support each other.

Starting Small

Often we have big goals in mind, whether that is to become a doctor, an aerospace engineer, or the boss of the company (if you notice, most goals have to do with what we are going to do or be in life). From the time we are small children, our parents, teachers, and other influencers talk to us about what we want to do when we grow up. As a kid, I remember dreaming about becoming a professional football player or a movie stuntman. Most pick some type of profession they see on a TV or YouTube program, or harbor fantasies about becoming a professional athlete. There are some children and young adults I have met who set more realistic goals, such as becoming a firefighter, teacher, or soldier.

This is where the positive speech I talked about in the previous chapter is so important. Parents, when you hear your children expressing goals for the future, encouragement is vital.

Help them dream big and reach for the stars, and help them grasp that the need to achieve small ones as they progress toward a bigger goal. Besides, it's much easier to reach the small ones along the way.

The wisdom of this step-by-step approach appears in the Bible. When Jesus told the parable about the shrewd steward, He said, "If you are faithful in little things, you will be faithful in large ones. But if you are dishonest in little things, you won't be honest with greater responsibilities" (Luke 16:10, NLT). In other words, God builds up believers by starting them out with a small responsibility. As we grow and improve, he increases our responsibility. In raising our children, we must establish the foundation of setting small goals in order to reach the big goal.

The government has already established this concept through the educational system. We start with kindergarten, move on to the first grade and the second, with the ultimate goal to reach the twelfth grade and graduate from high school. Even during these years, there are gradual steps, with classes broken down into quarters or semesters, and even smaller increments. Alongside the main goal, these small steps help you stay on track and determine where you're at and where you're going.

In recent years, electric cars have attracted increasing attention. One carmaker, Tesla Motors, manufactures a model S that has a range of more than 270 miles.[1] Yet if I set out to travel from Kennewick, Washington to Los Angeles, California—a distance of more than one thousand miles—I would have to establish small goals, particularly locating electric refueling sites along the way. When we set small goals, it encourages us and helps us get prepared to meet the next goal.

Although I have two master's degrees, I recognize that college is not for everyone. Still, regardless of your field, chances are you can get better equipped to advance by setting realistic goals to make yourself more marketable by developing skills that other people need and are willing to pay for what you know and can do.

Planning for the Future

Establishing goals is essentially planning for your future. And by achieving small goals, you motivate yourself to achieve the larger goal. When you teach your children to set goals, you are helping lay a strong foundation. In the previous chapter, I talked about the wisdom of working as a team to help your child get a glass of milk. While the child's ultimate goal was to pour a glass of milk, they didn't understand their abilities and lack of adequate strength to pour the milk. So as a parent, you taught them how they could achieve the goal through teamwork, and over time, they built up confidence and strength to pour their own milk.

This may seem trivial, but it applies to countless other examples. If your goal is to run a marathon, it will take training. If you're poor shape, you may have to start by walking a half mile as you gradually work your way up to running a mile. Once you do that, you can shoot for two miles. Setting the small goals is a way to reach the ultimate goal of twenty-six-plus miles. Without them, you will never reach the large one.

Writing Them Down

Writing down your goals is a powerful tool. This not only helps you remind yourself of your goal, but to visualize it. So if your goal is to be Green Beret, you must first set small goals. You would start with "Green Beret," and then list the requirements to achieve that. That includes holding a high school diploma, scoring high academic marks on the Armed Services Vocational Aptitude Battery (ASVAB) test, joining the Army, passing basic training, passing advanced infantry training, passing airborne training, passing Special Forces assessment and selection, passing the qualification course, and finally passing language training. If all you do is set your eyes on the prize of Green Beret status, that list will overwhelm you. But as I proved, by approaching it one step at a time, you can make it. Doing so will mean breaking those smaller goals into smaller steps. For example, learning what the requirements of the ASVAB test are and whether you need to take more math or grammar classes before graduating from high school. These are all small goals that you must accomplish just to be able talk to the Army recruiter and pass the ASVAB.

When you write down your goals and track your progress, reaching them builds confidence. When I would train people in martial arts or military tactics, I would assess where they were at—their present abilities and where they hoped to progress. Then I would give them attainable goals as I taught them what I knew that they could do. This built up their confidence for the next level. Once they achieved that and gained more confidence, their abilities increased. As their abilities increased, they moved closer to their primary goal until they achieved it.

One reason for writing down goals is to give them substance and move beyond the daydream stage. Too many people treat goals like some far-off dream, which is usually something that cannot be obtained. As a kid, I dreamed about becoming a professional football player, but I never established a roadmap of making that dream come true. Academics represented the roadblock along the way; I never thought I'd be smart enough to go to college and play football there, a necessary step to reaching the NFL. While that meant it only qualified as a daydream, I did set a realistic goal of becoming a police officer.

Since I didn't know what it took to be one, I researched the subject in order to develop a plan to get me where I wanted to go. It included ideas of what would make me marketable. Namely, why would XYZ Police Department want to hire me over other candidates? I talked to a few police officers and visited a police station to talk to someone in the human resources department. I shared my goal with that person and he told me what they were looking for, adding that I was a bit young (twenty-one). He suggested I join the Army Rangers or Navy SEALs (at that time, you could not join Special Forces straight off the street; you had to be in the military first). I listened, but along the way, I set new goals. After talking to recruiters from the Army and the Navy, I chose the Army.

Goals Change

The fact I never became a cop shows a simple reality about setting goals: they may change. When I enlisted, I never knew much about the military. Even though two of my brothers joined, I didn't come from a military family or grow up in that environment. One brother served in the Marines, but he never talked much about it after he came home. The other joined the Army, but didn't complete basic training. Still, when I made it to basic training, we often sang cadences about all the elite forces in the Army—such as "I want to be an airborne ranger." Over time, I learned more about special operations from other soldiers and my drill sergeants.

Once, while I was waiting to see an officer, a soldier sat down next to me. Immediately noticing the Green Beret and Special Forces tab on his left shoulder, I asked him if he liked it. "Yes, I do!" he replied. Before he could say anything more, he got called for his appointment. Although I didn't learn much that day about the Green Berets, I heard the enthusiasm echoing through his voice and the excitement shining in his eyes. That day, I thought about changing my goal from police officer. Over the first few years in the Army, I achieved status as a qualified sniper, scout reconnaissance specialist, and an Army Ranger. Two years into my enlistment, I realized my goal had changed. Now that I knew more about what active duty entailed, I decided that I liked the military and didn't want to leave after my first tour ended. So I set my eyes on becoming a Green Beret. The Special Forces training academy—Special Warfare Center and School—was just down the road from me in Fort Bragg, North Carolina. I talked to a Special Forces recruiter, determined the requirements, and signed up for training. The fact that my primary goal changed along the way didn't diminish my accomplishment.

Over the years, my academic goals also changed. My progress toward a bachelor's degree, and then advanced degrees, has come gradually. I achieved one goal and built my self-confidence, then established a new goal, built more confidence, and set out for another. At first, I wanted my bachelor's degree, something that looked like an impossible dream during my high school years. Later, when God directed me to enter the ministry, I knew I needed an education if I planned to teach others. So, I set out to obtain my master's degree in ministry. Yet I have another goal in mind. To enhance my understanding of the Bible, by studding Hebrew and the culture of the people in the Bible.

My studies of Scripture have convinced me that God wants us to establish plans and goals and count the cost of these goals. We must make sure our goals are attainable, that we can achieve our plans, and that they complement each other. As Jesus asked while teaching the crowds: "For which of you, intending to build a tower, does not sit down first and count the cost, whether he has enough to finish it" (Luke 14:28). Not only does He tell us to count the cost to ensure that we have enough finances and other support to complete the project, we must determine if this is a necessity. Sometimes we can be over-trained or overqualified for a task, which is why you must make sure what you are doing benefits your goal. When my son was preparing to go to college, I told him, "Talk regularly to your academic advisors. Make sure you're not taking extra classes or wasting your time and money. Don't do something that is not going to help you reach your goal, which is graduating sooner rather than later."

When Is It Too Late?

There a simple answer to the above question: when you're dead. You should never stop setting goals. It is never too late to start either. Too often people, particularly in middle age or beyond, think, "This is the way my life is going to turn out. This is the path I've established." However, if you continue to plan and set goals, you are setting a foundation for others to follow. This applies whether you a parent modeling behavior for your children, an aunt or uncle teaching your nieces and nephews, a grandparent advising grandchildren, or a supervisor influencing your employees.

One of my favorite stories about an Army veteran who decided it wasn't too late to embark on a new career is Dr. Mike Moore, a family medicine resident at Madigan Army Medical Center in Tacoma, Washington. Now in his fifties, the Army Major decided to enroll at Pacific Northwest University of Health Sciences in his late forties. That, despite meaning he had to listen to lectures from professors who were younger than him, alongside students his children's age.

In reporting on Moore's unusual choice during his second year of medical training, CNN noted that stories about mid-life career transitions often involve stressed-out professionals who quit their job to pursue a passion like baking cupcakes or opening a café: "Seldom do they involve a more rigorous route—like becoming a doctor in your 40s and 50s. Medicine is a pressure-packed field that requires between seven and 11 years of training, including post-medical school residencies with 80-hour workweeks. Future doctors like Moore who make unlikely career choices are called nontraditional students, and they are increasingly attractive candidates for medical schools. 'Some of them have become the most desirable applicants,' said David Muller, dean for medical education at Mount Sinai School of Medicine."[2]

Nor is Dr. Moore alone. According to the American Osteopathic Association (AOA), in 2012, students in doctor of osteopathy programs were as old as sixty-one—the same age as Clarence Nicodemus when he earned his degree in 2004 from the Michigan State University College of Osteopathic Medicine in East Lansing, Michigan. Several dozen students enrolled in school in 2012 were expected to graduate at age fifty or older. That year, the AOA's roster of living physicians contains more than two hundred people who were at least fifty when they graduated.[3]

As noteworthy as those accomplishments are, consider the story about Lela Burden of Norfolk, Virginia, who received her high school diploma in June of 2014—at the age of 111. Schools had temporarily shut down nearly a century before during a flu pandemic, and by the time they reopened, she was working two jobs and took decades to return and complete her education. A month before graduation, as she celebrated her latest birthday, she told a TV station, "I'm not old yet. I'm still a young lady."[4]

Such stories illustrate that it is never too late to set goals. With them, you will stay active and maintain a purpose in life. Instead of looking for the nearest recliner or golf course (which is a sure way to die young) when you turn sixty, you will still have things to achieve. The Bible is full of stories of people who continued setting goals, whether that was someone like eighty-year-old Moses returning to lead Israel out of captivity, or Abraham fathering a child at the age of one hundred. The fascinating part of Abraham's story (which many people overlook) is that after the birth of his son, Isaac, he fathered *six more* children with his second wife, Keturah (see Genesis 25:1–2).

Setting Goals into Action

If you are driving somewhere, you will either pull out a roadmap or program your destination into your GPS device so you can establish a route to reach your destination. However, many of us spend more time planning our vacation than we do planning our retirement. I don't mean "retire" as in sit around all day and do nothing, but what course you plan to follow once you aren't subject to deadlines, meetings, phone calls, and other pressures. That may mean starting a new business, turning a hobby or avocation into a fulltime pursuit, mentoring young professionals, or volunteering at community organizations.

Still, it is important to establish the foundation for your children of planning for retirement. Some of you may think that is ludicrous: "Why am I going to talk to a seven-year-old kid retirement? They don't even have an allowance yet." However, you may remember me discussing the Jewish people in chapter 2 and how they train their children from a very young age. Setting a foundation for your children's future includes planning for their retirement, even though they may not have any concept of what you mean at the time.

Think of it as building a house; when you set the foundation, you may not even know what it will look like when it's completed. Yet you build the foundation strong so it can withstand storms. Jesus addressed this in his "Sermon on the Mount:" "Therefore whoever hears these sayings of Mine, and does them, I will liken him to a wise man who built his house on the rock: and the rain descended, the floods came, and the winds blew and beat on that house; and it did not fall, for it was founded on the rock. But everyone who hears these sayings of Mine, and does not do them, will be like a foolish man who built his house on the sand: and the rain descended, the floods came, and the winds blew and beat on that house; and it fell. And great was its fall" (Mathew 7:24–27).

For us to be good stewards of our children, we must teach them in the ways they must go. In the words of Solomon: "Train up a child in the way he should go, and when he is old he will not depart from it" (Proverbs 22:6). Pastors often refer to this verse in reference to a belief in God and a relationship with Jesus Christ. However, this doesn't just apply to spirituality; it relates to everything else I have discussed in these pages. The foundation a parent establishes on education, morality, sexuality, positive speech, leadership, motivation, intimacy, and family will be part of their children's foundation for the remainder of their life. Our job is to equip our children with the foundation they need to be successful. It is their job to take what we have given them and do something with it. While our children will not always head in the direction we hope, when we establish a strong foundation, they will eventually do the right thing with it.

Choosing the Best Route

Goals and planning are our responsibility. The government may help you establish an educational goal, but the rest is up to you. What are your goals? Start with an overarching, big picture goal and smaller, attainable ones that can help you to reach it. Do the research so you understand what it is required to reach them. Then, set your path to get there, keeping in mind that the most direct route is not always the best one.

One time in the Army, a young sergeant accompanied me on a task to do land navigation. As we discussed it, he said, "You want to go the most direct route—down the valley and back up the other side." The sergeant thought going straight ahead would be quickest and the best way. I replied, "No, taking the ridge line around the valley will allow you to make the trip quicker and with less effort." He didn't believe me, so I told him, "Okay, you go your way, and I'll go mine, and we'll see who gets there first." To make a long story short, I was waiting for him on the other side as he trudged up the valley sweaty, tired, and frustrated. So remember to use wisdom when setting goals and making decisions. If you lack wisdom, seek some out. Remember, any plan is better than no plan.

Notes

1. https://www.teslamotors.com/models.
2. Madison Park, "Never too late to be a doctor," CNN, June 13, 3011, http://www.cnn.com/2011/HEALTH/06/13/mid.life.doctors/.
3. Carolyn Schierhorn, "Older medical students persist, leverage life

experience to achieve dreams," http://thedo.osteopathic.org/2013/06/older-medical-students-persist-leverage-life-experience-to-achieve-dreams/.
4. Reed Andrews, "Woman graduates from high school at 111-years-old," WTKR-TV, http://wtkr.com/2014/06/17/woman-graduates-from-high-sch

CHAPTER 10
The Foundation of Forgiveness

I am concluding with a look at the foundational concept of forgiveness because it is one of the keys to recovering from past struggles. The reason I made forgiveness the last chapter is because it is the last thing we do, it should be the first thing we do, but for some reason, we always seem to forgive others as the last thing we do! You can never move on to a brighter future if you are bound by the chains of the past. As with the root issues I discussed in chapter 2, the need to forgive often goes back to childhood. No matter what the identity of the person who hurt us—father, mother, relative, stranger, or family friend—refusing to forgive the offender means that mixture of lemon with apple tree will sprout the fruit of bitterness. It will continue to aggravate and frustrate you until you learn to forgive.

Forgiveness is often the final step in overcoming the past. Victims of abuse (remember, I was one) will often do everything to heal from their wounds, whether that involves going to regular therapy sessions; commiserating with friends; self-medicating with drugs, alcohol, or even food; or trying other forms of escape. People will do everything possible to fix the issue on their own, but neglect the essential step of forgiveness. I have heard people snarl, "I've forgiven him, but I'll never forget." What that means is they haven't forgiven. You may never forget; certain scars inflict indelible scars on our soul. When I say you should forget as you forgive, I mean to lay the offenses aside and not rehearse them, stew in them, or allow them to keep you locked in a state of perpetual uproar. Constantly reminding yourself of the *bad deeds this person did* to you and *how wronged you are* will keep you from ever getting over it.

Sadly, some of those who cling to bitterness and unforgiveness call themselves followers of Christ. This in spite of numerous Bible verses that talk about forgiveness. One example is Mark 11:25 (ESV), where Jesus said, "And whenever you stand praying, forgive, if you have anything against anyone, so that your Father also who is in heaven may forgive you your trespasses." Matthew 6:14–15 is another: "For if you forgive men their trespasses, your heavenly Father will also forgive you. But if you do not forgive men their trespasses, neither will your Father forgive your trespasses." Then there is the instructive passage where Peter asked Jesus how many times he should forgive someone and Christ replies, "I do not say to you, up to seven times, but up to seventy times seven" (Matthew 18:22). What Jesus meant was not that we can forgive someone 490 times and then unload on the offender. He was saying we must continue to forgive just as His Father has forgiven each of us: without boundaries.

Forgiveness is the ability to stop feeling angry or resentful toward someone else for an offense they've done to you. In the rest of this chapter, I will examine some reasons we should forgive and how it affects us.

Life Is Too Short

If we go through life and don't forgive, the resulting bitterness will surface physically. It will be like calcium deposits that can harden and cause kidney stones, hardening of the arteries, or cardiovascular disease. We can literally stew ourselves into a debilitating illness. The stress of an unforgiving heart can literally kill you. When you lug around the burden of hatred and unforgiveness, this hardening becomes your down fall. Nor is this bitterness a solitary endeavor. It affects your relationships with others, be that your immediately family, relatives, friends, or co-workers. It will reap serious damage later in life too. People who grow older and harbor unforgiveness in their heart often become reclusive and separated from others at the very time they need a social support network to help them deal with the frailties and fears of old age.

A person hidden away and out of contact with other humans is not living a life filled with grace and truth. Isolation leaves people susceptible to incredible loneliness and depression. The question each of us must face is: How long will I allow this bitterness to hold me prisoner? How long will I allow hatred for another (who may not even know of my anger—or may even be dead) to destroy me? Ironically, the person you are nursing a grudge against and seething with resentment toward has likely forgotten about the incident. The only person you're hurting is yourself. Only when you recognize that unforgiveness has trapped you in a cycle of misery can you start to change. You may have heard the truism that the first sign of an alcoholic or drug addict overcoming their problem is when they realize they have an addiction. When you are hurting and recognize the root of your pain comes from your unforgiveness toward the person that hurt you in the past, it represents the first step toward being able to forgive.

As someone who suffered great trauma in childhood, I can assure you that you are most likely the only person affected by this deep-seated agony that troubles you and—to use a familiar term—keeps you enslaved. Life is far too short to live it in unhappiness and misery. My experience is that some people will accept you for who you are and love you. Others will not. The very reason some people like you will be the reason others dislike you. The point is that you no control over how anyone else feels. If someone is angry at you or refuses to accept you for who they are, allow them to carry that burden. It's not yours! Live each day as if it were your last. Live for the Lord. Live to enjoy happiness and refuse to get trapped in misery.

Whenever you forgive whoever harmed you in the past, you can start to change not only your outlook about the past, but your vision for the future. Adopting an optimistic outlook can help you become a better, happier, healthier person. Forgiveness is one of the keys to happiness. In the dozens of places I have traveled during my lifetime, I have encountered numerous people who never learn to forgive. As a result, they reach the last chapter of their lives caught in a cycle of hatred, bitterness, and unhappiness. They are clinging to their burdens and clasping on to unforgiveness over something that happened in childhood—fifty, sixty, or seventy years earlier! They are not only unhappy, they're pessimistic, always looking for the bad in other people or expecting a negative outcome in every situation.

Wearing these kinds of blinders prevents a person from experiencing any joy in life. As anyone in their senior years can assure you, life will blink by so fast you'll be shocked at the speed. The more quickly you forgive, the quicker you will able to find the peace, love, and happiness that has eluded you for so long. The Lord's Prayer in Matthew 6 is also called The Model Prayer because in these words Jesus modeled the perfect way for people to approach His Heavenly Father, including verse 12: "And forgive us our debts, as we forgive our debtors." We forgive the debt—the harm someone caused us—because God the Father has forgiven even greater wrongs on our part. If we expect God to forgive us, we must learn to forgive others. Sure, they may not deserve your forgiveness. But you didn't deserve God's.

Health Benefits

Not only can unforgiveness make your life a misery, it can damage your health. With each passing day, the bitterness and resentment that stem from unforgiveness will raise your level of anxiety, increase your blood pressure, and contribute to frustration, which will worsen your state of health. However, if you want to decrease your anxiety, stress levels, and agitation, then learn to forgive. The person you will bless through such action is not the object of your unforgiveness—it's you. Forgiveness and happiness co-exist for your well-being! When you learn to be at peace with yourself and reduce your anxiety, along with your blood pressure, it can positively affect your weight and other factors.

This observation is borne out by researchers at Harvard University. They cite how a vast body of scientific literature reveals that negative emotions can harm the body, with serious, sustained stress (or fear) altering one's biological systems. Over time, this creates a wear and tear on the body and eventually can lead to such ailments as heart disease, stroke, or diabetes. What's more, they say that chronic anger and anxiety can harm cardiac functions, hasten hardening of the arteries, and increasing inflammation in your system, which causes all kinds of health problems.

Going back to my observation about the apple tree in chapter 2, these professors point out how early childhood disruptions can cause "toxic stress," the kind that causes negative impacts on the brain and other organs. Laura Kubansky, a professor of human development, led a study of more than six thousand people ages twenty-five to seventy-four, which lasted for twenty years. She found that things like enthusiasm, hopefulness, and emotional balance appear to reduce the risk of heart disease: "It looks like there is a benefit of positive mental health that goes beyond the fact that you're not depressed."[1]

In other words, happiness promotes enthusiasm, optimism, positive self-esteem create better friendships and other interpersonal relationships. The bottom line: forgiveness equals happiness and happiness equals health.

Finding Freedom

Not only will forgiving those who hurt you free you from the burdens of your past; it will enable you to move forward in life. This freedom is one of the most important parts of forgiveness because it allows you to draw closer to God. You will be free to have a loving relationship with the Lord and Savior, Jesus Christ, because you won't be held back by chains of bitterness that block your prayers and hinder your spirit. If you don't allow yourself to forgive, then you aren't allowing yourself to be free.

Having worked through the situation, I know how long it takes and the grueling nature of the battle. Reaching a deep, long-lasting condition of forgiveness doesn't happen overnight. Just being able to forgive yourself—if you bear even a hint of responsibility—for the bad blood lingering from a contentious situation can hold you back. For years, I carried around the burden of my previous divorce. I still struggle occasionally with guilt over the past separation from my children. It took a long time to learn to forgive myself and allow myself to be the best father I can be, despite the circumstances. Even though the divorce happened many years ago and my children are grown, at times I still feel sad and sorrowful over those lost years. It wasn't their fault that their mother and I separated and ultimately got divorced; I only wish I had grasped then how deeply a divorce traumatizes an entire family. Unfortunately, I hurt them and can only pray that they forgive me and their mother for those circumstances.

I had to also learn to forgive my mother for the bad example that she gave me when it came to commitment and marriage. Within the past few years, I had to learn to forgive myself for repeating the cycle that I learned from Mom. Having done this, I can assure you that the pain of not forgiving yourself, or someone else, will hold you down. It will prevent you from enjoying positive relationships in life, which—as I pointed out in the previous section—affects your health.

Forgiveness is a key to vitality in life. When you are free to be happy, you are free to enjoy this short life to the fullest. Learn to be free, which will come from forgiveness. Drawing away from burdens and closer to God, and relying on His sovereign will for your life, will take you much further than you can make it on your own.

Allowing Abuse

Because of the abuse I suffered in childhood, and counseling with other abuse victims, I know that parents can often be burdened with unforgiveness when abuse happened to their child. Like a leader on a battlefield when one of their soldiers dies, they can spend the rest of their life reliving that horrible event over and over in their head. As if they could somehow change the past, they try to figure out what they could have done differently to prevent such a tragedy. Parents do this not only when child is abused by a relative or close friend, but in other circumstances. They agonize endlessly, i.e., *"If I* would have only picked a different babysitter..." "I should *never have left* my son or daughter alone with their uncle..." "*If only* I hadn't taken that second job..."

Many spend the rest of their days not only trying to determine how they could have gone so wrong, but blaming themselves for the tragedy. In the same way a battlefield leader can't prevent every loss, the truth is that it's likely there's nothing the parent could have done. Since we're all human, we all make mistakes. We can spend countless hours reevaluating and second-guessing our past decisions. With the benefit of hindsight, we can always come up with better reasons, theories, and solutions, but the reality is that we did the best we could under the circumstances. With the knowledge we had at the time, we made the best decisions we could and the best choices we could make.

If you are a parent who is endlessly replaying "What if?" scenarios in your mind, you likely have come up with a thousand ways of how you could have prevented such a catastrophe. As a result, you're not able to forgive yourself for your child's tragedy. But I can tell you from personal experience that during the occasions I was molested, there is little my parents could have done. Molesters are cunning predators who do their best to isolate innocent victims. They start out innocently—playing games, taking a child out for ice cream, spending time with them—as they build trust and a relationship. They are patient as they hatch their diabolical plots.

So as a molestation victim, I would tell any parents of other victims to stop blaming yourself. Forgive yourself and the offender. We make good and bad decisions in life. The goal is to learn to minimize repeating the bad ones.

Why Is It So Difficult?

Many people don't understand the nature of forgiveness or how to go about it. Often people will say they have forgiven something when what they really do is pack it away in a suitcase. Finally, after they stuff it so full it can't hold anything else, it explodes like someone put a stick of dynamite in the suitcase. Any married couple knows the feeling. A spouse does something, and we get upset with them. After the arguments each apologizes and expresses sorrow. But a month later, we get into another argument and bring up the past argument. That prompts a surprised look as the spouse says, "But I thought that was over. You said you forgave me!" In reality, we didn't forgive. We set it aside, to use it at a later date for revenge.

As a pastor and counselor who deals regularly with people who can't forgive and has researched the Bible in depth, I think a primary reason humans have such a hard time forgiving is because it hurts. It cuts deep into our inner being. When you have a festering wound you have to pick out the scab (a bit grotesque of an image, but true). When someone hurts us, it can create a festering wound that is scabbed over, just waiting to be picked at. One reason we can allow the wound to fester: we don't feel the other person received their rightful punishment. They have walked around for the last month, free of all responsibility for the hurt they caused. Now we want to pay them back and tell them what they've done to us and how our heart has been hurting. It doesn't help alleviate our anger if our spouse or partner responds, "Why are you always bringing up the past?" Indeed, it exacerbates the problem and indicates how the previous fight did not get resolved. Obviously one person walked away happy, but not the other.

So if we want to forgive, we must first learn what forgiveness is and how to go about it. Forgiveness is not letting the person off completely and exonerating them of all responsibility. There should be some type of reconciliation between the two parties so the harm that has been done can be resolved, allowing each person to move on. I compare it to Jesus Christ going to the cross, where He became the atoning sacrifice for all.

Atonement is making an offense right so you can carry on as normal. If you get a speeding ticket, you make atonement to society by paying a fine for breaking the law. Once you have made things right, society forgives you of wrongdoing and you are able to drive without further penalty. So the reconciliation process is for the one who offends and for the ones who are offended. This means there should be some type of atonement so both parties are free of guilt. When you forgive someone, that doesn't mean that you should continue going back to go back to that person and have them continue to violate you. If that's the case, it was a one-way atonement. You extended the person forgiveness but they didn't reciprocate.

For example, a man in ministry treated us shabbily—even after we supported his church financially. The final straw took place when the pastor scolded my wife and me because she asked for prayer at a time when he felt it was inappropriate time. I disagreed; after all, she had raised her hand during a meeting and only asked her question after he called on her. Consequently, we left that church. Nor did he ever call to apologize and try to make amends.

One day as I drove by a coffee shop, I felt God putting a conviction in my heart to stop by the church and try to reconcile. Through a considerable amount of prayer (and a lot of resistance on my part initially), I obeyed. Stopping at the church, I went in to meet with him and apologize for any offense that I caused and asked if we could reconcile our relationship. We talked for a while, it was all cordial. Prior to leaving, I asked if we would ever get together again and develop our relationship. "No," he replied, "I'm okay." Sometimes forgiveness is a one-way street. However, if we do our part, it will set us free. Because I took a step to forgive, I don't fret over what happened or his reaction.

Learn to Let Go

Another area where we may feel resentment when we forgive is if that person does not receive what we see as "just" punishment, or at least acknowledges their part in the situation. This is where we must learn to let go. As with the example I just covered about that pastor, I have clung to resentment for him because I felt that he didn't reciprocate in forgiveness or express the least concern for the reconciliation process. However, if I had held on to that, it means I would have not truly forgiven him. And it would cause me more problems in the future. To settle this in our mind, we must acknowledge that God is the One who sits in judgment and will hold that person accountable.

Sometimes we can wrongly assume that the other person didn't forgive or handle their part fairly, but in fact they did. We must acknowledge that we can misread people or circumstances. We do not have the ability to read minds, spirits, or hearts; only God has that power. It is not our responsibility to make them to reconcile with us. It is our responsibility to ensure that we do our part—then leave the rest up to God. We cannot control other people and we are not responsible for them. We can only control ourselves and be held responsible for our own actions.

Here it is also worth mentioning "enforced" forgiveness. You likely remember childhood when you did something mean to your brother, sister, or a kid in the neighborhood and your mom or dad caught you. They typically would force you apologize for your actions. Quite often as children we would apologize, but not really mean it. Now, the person that we apologized to (or if we were the recipient of such an apology) thought all was forgiven and went away happy. Yet we knew it wasn't sincere, even if the person who received the apology accepted it as a sign of reconciliation. My point: we are only responsible for our actions and can feel reconciled even if the other person won't reconcile with us.

Also, we must not offer forgiveness unless we are truly ready to forgive. Offering forced forgiveness like we did in childhood is only providing lip service. If you find yourself in a situation where you're struggling to extend authentic forgiveness, the answer is to pray. The Bible teaches in Psalms: "God is our refuge and strength, a very present help in trouble" (Psalm 46:1, ESV). Proverbs 3:5–6 teaches that we should trust in the Lord and lean on His understanding; He will direct our path and show us the way to go. Remember forgiveness starts with us; we must make a mental decision to forgive. As I mentioned in the chapter on the foundation of speech, we think it, speak it, believe it, and then act on it. When we learn to forgive, we are setting the foundation for a better life.

Notes

1. "Happiness and Health," Harvard T. H. Chan School of Public Health, Winter 2011, http://www.hsph.harvard.edu/news/magazine/happiness-stress-hea

1. About the Author

The inspiration to tell his story can be accredited to his wife, Teresa; Gordon states that she believed his story would not only help others, but inspire them as well, regardless if they have experienced trauma within their lives. Gordon's fractured past did not hold him back from becoming a former U.S. Army Sniper, Army Ranger, and Army Special Forces (Green Beret). With his relentless desire to overcome and his relationship with Jesus Christ, the challenges he faced in academia did not hold him back from achieving multiple degrees. He holds a bachelor's degree in Business administration, a Master's degree in Ministry, and a Master's degree in Leadership. Prior to retiring from the Army, Gordon was called by God to change careers and start a new career with God. Gordon is currently the senior pastor of New Heritage Church in Kennewick, WA, and is now a warrior for God.

www.ingramcontent.com/pod-product-compliance
Lightning Source LLC
LaVergne TN
LVHW051225070526
838200LV00057B/4606